Y0-BCR-260

TABLE OF CONTENTS

PREFACE

Forensic pathology may be horrifying to some. Even among pathologists, only a few choose forensics as a career. Yet, many people find themselves vicariously attracted to the subject through novels, TV shows, and trials.

We believe that the horror and attraction is captured by an etching, entitled *La Morgue, Paris*. Completed in 1854 by Charles Meryon, considered one of the greatest architectural etchers of all times, it depicts a naked woman's body removed from the Seine by two rescuers. The scene is shocking to a woman and child who shield their faces as a policeman points to the steps of the morgue. The paradox depicted in this etching is that through the death of this woman, a tragedy for her family, artists and physicians will, through an autopsy, study anatomy and whatever her death has to offer. Consequently, from the despair of another's tragedy comes hope, understanding, and knowledge. A mixed mood of despair and hope is captured in this etching.

For us, *La Morgue, Paris* signifies our intent in writing this book: to bring understanding and knowledge to those who frequently deal with forensic deaths but lack formal forensic training. Although a Guide to Forensic Pathology is intended primarily for death investigators, it may also be used by anyone who wishes to learn more about forensic pathology such as medical students, pathology residents, pathologists, coroners, medical examiners, homicide detectives, and other forensic experts. Readers wanting a more detailed discussion of particular topics in forensic pathology and death investigation should refer to one of the following texts or journals:

Texts:

1. Adelson L: "The Pathology of Homicide," Charles C. Thomas, 1971.

2. Spitz W, Fischer R (eds): "Medicolegal Investigation of Death," 3rd Ed Charles C. Thomas, 3rd Edition, 1994.
3. DiMaio V, DiMaio D: "Forensic Pathology," Elsevier, 1990.
4. DiMaio V: "Gunshot Wounds," Elsevier, 1989.
5. Wecht C (ed): "Forensic Sciences," Matthew Bender, 1981 with periodic updates.

Journals:

1. *Forensic Sciences*
2. *American Journal of Forensic Sciences*
3. *Forensic Sciences International*

The book had its origins in our former work *Case Studies in Forensic Pathology.* We decided to reorganize the overall structure without dramatically changing the content or style. Case studies are now contained in their own section. Several additions have been made. The introduction has been expanded with Guidelines for the Death Scene Investigator by Mary Fran Ernst. Separate sections have been included on DNA Testing and Helpful Hints in Testifying. Forty photographs from Dr. Dix's personal collection have also been included in Appendix A.

As with any project of this magnitude, gratitude can be extended to many. The authors wish to cite a few. First, John F. Townsend, MD, Chairman of Department of Pathology and Anatomical Sciences for allowing us to work on this project with his resources, and for his wisdom and humanitarianism. Second, Kirstie Calcutt, who helped tie this book together. Her diligence and patience were major factors in seeing this project completed. Her expertise in computer systems and illustrations were vital in the overall organization. Our gratitude extends beyond these pages. Third, the St. Louis Art Museum for giving us permission to use a copy of *La Morgue, Paris* for our cover. And finally, our students who provided useful suggestions for improving our *Case Studies* book. We hope they recongize that through the despair of their predecessors comes understanding and knowledge.

PART I
Introduction

History

Death investigation in the United States originated in England. As early as the 12th century, there was an elected coroner who protected the crown's interest from corrupt sheriffs. With time, the coroner's jurisdiction over financial matters gave way to investigating deaths. The power of these death investigators grew to the degree that they could arrest suspected criminals and the sheriff (in Missouri the coroner can still arrest the sheriff). The coroner was required to assemble a group of peers to judge a suspect's guilt or innocence. This functioned as an early form of the inquest, a proceeding still conducted in some jurisdictions. The group also considered the necessity of a postmortem examination (autopsy).

The word autopsy is derived from ancient Greek and literally means to view for oneself.[1] Its common usage, however, is the postmortem examination of a body, including both an external viewing and an internal dissection, to determine the cause of death and a description of any pathological changes. In ancient cultures this examination is also associated with philosophical and religious issues such as one's search and identification of the soul and understanding one's own mortality. Consequently, it is not known when the first autopsy was performed. King and Mechan provide a good review of the history of the autopsy.[2]

The original settlers brought this system to our country and it remained similar to the English system for many years. The first person called a medical examiner was appointed in Boston during the late 1870's. Neither the coroner nor the medical examiner had to be a forensic pathologist. The first citywide independent system for death investigation was established in New York City in 1918 and the first statewide system was developed in Maryland in 1939. There have been many changes throughout the country in death investigation during the ensuing decades.

Death investigation in the United States is performed differently from state to state and, in several states, from county to county. Some states have a statewide medical examiner system with trained forensic professionals. Other states retain the system of elected lay coroners who have little forensic or medical training. Except in a few states such as Missouri, in which medical examiners may be any type of physician, most medical examiners are forensic pathologists (see section about experts encountered in death investigation).

References:

1. Dorland's Illustrated Medical Dictionary, 28th Ed. Philadelphia, W.B. Saunders Co., 1994.
2. King L, Mechan M: A History of Autopsy: A Review. American Journal of Pathology 73: 514-544, 1973.

Experts Encountered In Death Investigation

Forensic Pathologist

Forensic pathology, a subspecialty in pathology, is the study of how and why people die. A physician who becomes a forensic pathologist first attends an approved pathology residency program and may spend three years in a strictly anatomic program or five years in a combined anatomic and clinical program. One or two additional years are devoted to studying the pathology of sudden, unexpected, natural death, as well as violent death, in one of approximately 30 approved forensic fellowship training programs throughout the country. Most programs are centered in major cities which have a large number of deaths from various causes. A forensic fellow studies how people die by: performing numerous autopsies; attending scene investigations; and studying the specialties of criminalistics, ballistics, serology, toxicology, anthropology, odontology, and radiology. The most important area of study is death investigation, but some forensic pathology programs also include examination of the living to determine physical and sexual abuse. After training, the pathologist is eligible to take a board certification examination in forensic pathology administered by the American Board of Pathology. There are fewer than 1,000 board certified forensic pathologists in the United States.

One definition of the word "forensic" means dealing with the courts and legal system. This definition describes two

3

important functions of a forensic pathologist: deciding how and why a person died, and defending and explaining these diagnoses in a courtroom. A forensic pathologist may be called as a witness by either the prosecution or the defense. The state, however, usually calls a pathologist since he performed the autopsy. Regardless of who calls a pathologist to testify, the testimony should be an unbiased account of opinions as to why a person died or was injured. Medical information must be presented to a jury as clearly as possible since they will decide whether an accused person is guilty or innocent. A forensic pathologist must be an expert in death investigation. The importance of an investigation in any death cannot be overemphasized. A scene investigation is probably more important than an autopsy. A thorough and complete investigation commonly leads an examiner to suspect the proper cause and manner of death prior to an autopsy. In many cases an autopsy is the only means to confirm what is already known and to collect specimens. Well-trained investigators are an integral part in any forensic jurisdiction. The importance of investigation will become more evident throughout the text.

Most full-time forensic pathologists work in either a medical examiner's or coroner's office located in larger cities. These offices may operate as separate departments or divisions of other city, county, or state agencies. For example, many are under the Attorney General's Office or Departments of Health or Public Safety. These offices vary in jurisdiction in each state and usually investigate traumatic, sudden, unexpected, or suspicious deaths. They are also directly or indirectly connected to crime labs which have experts in serology, trace evidence, toxicology, and ballistics.

Medical Examiner or Coroner

The central character in medicolegal death investigation is the medical examiner or coroner. This person gathers information concerning the scene and autopsy in order to rule on both the cause and manner of death. A medical examiner or coroner may not perform the autopsy. In such cases, a pathologist's findings are combined with the investigation to render a final opinion. Larger jurisdictions have their own investigators while smaller ones either rely on the local law enforcement agency or perform their own investigations.

Death Investigator

Larger jurisdictions may have their own investigators who receive an initial call to go to a death scene and make an evaluation. They report to a medical examiner or pathologist performing the autopsy. Their job is important because they work closely with law enforcement at a scene and obtain all necessary information about a decedent. They gather relevant medical history as well as talk to witnesses and relatives about a decedent's last whereabouts and circumstances surrounding his death. This information is significant in determining the cause and manner of death because using autopsy information alone may lead to an inaccurate conclusion.

Crime Scene Technician

The crime scene technician's job begins after a body is discovered. This expert is specially trained and usually a member of local law enforcement or a state-wide investigative unit. The technician's expertise includes: photographing and diagramming the death scene; collecting all potentially important evidence in an investigation, such as blood, hair, fiber samples and weapons; and recovering fingerprints and other prints, such as those from shoes and tires.

Criminalist

This is the expert most people consider when evidence is sent to a forensic laboratory for analysis. The criminalist receives training in such areas as questioned documents, ballistics, serology, and toxicology. Most criminalists work with evidence (e.g., blood, bullets, fingerprints, ammunition) and trace evidence (e.g., fibers and hair, soil, glass, and impressions) left by other objects.

A ballistics expert can match a bullet from the victim to a test-fired weapon. This is accomplished by analyzing both a recovered bullet and a test-fired bullet under a comparison microscope. Every handgun and rifle has spiral grooves (lands-and-grooves) in the barrel which gives a bullet better trajectory. All weapons of similar type and manufacturer have the same number of lands-and-grooves. Therefore, an examiner can tell the type and make of gun which fired a bullet if it is not completely deformed. If a bullet has a metal jacket, such as copper, it will leave impressions from grooves that would not be seen on lead. The base of the cartridge can be examined for the firing pin impression which can also be matched to a particular gun. Shotgun pellets cannot be matched to a particular gun because there are no grooves in a shotgun barrel. The pellets are weighed for determination of size, and the lead composition is determined and compared to an unfired specimen.

A ballistics expert also performs tests for the presence of gunpowder residue on a suspect or the decedent. Such testing is helpful in determining if a person fired a weapon or was close to one when it was discharged. The tests will be of little value if the hands are not tested within approximately six hours of the firing, or if the alleged assailant washes his hands prior to the test.

This expert can test a variety of other materials such as soil for its component elements and glass for its fragility and direction of impact. Impressions, such as from a shoe sole or tire tread, can be matched to referenced products. Paint chips can be analyzed for their components and compared to the paint used by known manufacturers. Manufacturers of automobiles, for instance, keep accurate records of the paint used on each make and model. Volatile liquids, such as gasoline or paint thinner, can be determined from a suspected arson case.

Serologist

A serologist analyzes fluids such as blood, urine, or semen removed from a scene. If a specimen is not decomposed it can be compared to the blood types of all parties involved in an investigation. Blood need not be fluid to be of value; dried specimens, removed from weapons or other objects, are also useful. Occasionally, specific typing cannot be performed and a serologist can only determine whether or not such blood was human. DNA fingerprinting has also become very helpful. Everyone has unique DNA except identical twins. White blood cells can be examined for their DNA content and compared to other specimens. If a test uses strict scientific methodology, the results can be extremely valuable. DNA testing is also performed on hair, semen, and saliva.

A serologist can test semen for the presence and motility of sperm. Sperm remain motile for up to 24 hours before they die. Vaginal, oral, and anal swabs can also be tested for the presence of seminal fluid and sperm.

Secretors are people who secrete their blood type in their body fluids. Approximately 80% of all individuals are secretors. Blood, urine, sweat, saliva, and semen contain an individual's blood type. Most people are type O, followed in order of decreasing frequency by A, B, and AB.

Questioned Documents Examiner

This person is able to analyze handwriting. He can determine whether or not a suspect actually wrote the document in question. Paper can be evaluated for its ingredients and age, and ink can be analyzed for its chemical composition. Writing instruments such as typewriters or pens can also be evaluated.

Toxicologist

A toxicologist evaluates organs and fluids from an autopsy and a scene for the presence or absence of drugs and chemicals. The types of pills or powders found on suspects can also be determined. Most common drugs of abuse and poisons can be readily discovered and quantitated. Every drug and chemical, however, does not appear in a routine drug screen. A pathologist and investigator must consult with a toxicologist if any unusual drugs or poisons are suspected. They should also tell a toxicologist which prescribed or illegal drugs a decedent had taken. Drugs and medicines from a scene should be recovered for analysis if needed.

A report is produced after testing is completed. Generally, a toxicologist should refrain from giving an opinion as to the cause and manner of death because he is not aware of all information from an investigation and autopsy. It is a pathologist's job to gather all the data and arrive at an explanation of a victim's death.

Anthropologist

Anthropologists study bones and determine race, gender, and age range in most cases. Complete skeletons are easier to work with and yield more accurate results than partial skeletons. Some anthropologists specialize in reconstructing facial detail from skull bones and identifying unknown skeletons. Anthropologists, however, should not make a positive identification from bones alone unless other material is available for comparison, such as an x-ray or a detailed medical report. Anthropologists have been known to evaluate specific bony injuries in order to help with determining a cause of death.

Odontologist (Dentist)

A bite mark on a victim or an assailant can be matched to the person making the bite. An expert who can analyze and interpret this data undergoes specialized training. Prior to making molds and photographs of the marks, an odontologist swabs the area to remove any saliva. The blood type of an offender can be determined if the offender is a secretor. An odontologist is also an important consultant when positive identification is required. Only fingerprints are more commonly used than dental comparisons in identifying unknown bodies when visual identification cannot be made and a body is still intact.

Radiologist

A radiologist's expertise is used frequently by a medical examiner's office. Comparisons of antemortem to postmortem radiographs often aid in decedent identification. These analyses are very important when a decedent cannot be identified by fingerprints or dental exams. A radiologist is also consulted for evaluating bony abnormalities in cases of suspected child abuse.

Entomologist

Entomologists identify the type of insects at a scene and the age of larvae. They know which insects are prevalent at any particular time of the year and how long it takes before eggs are laid on a body. This information helps in determining the length of time a body remained in a particular location. It does not tell an examiner how long a person was dead, since a body found in one location may be transported to another.

Accident Reconstructionist

These specialists are usually policemen, highway patrolmen, or forensic engineers who have advanced training in recreating motor vehicle accidents. They can determine a motor vehicle's speed at the time of an accident and how vehicles react after impact. They may also determine a body's location in a vehicle prior to impact.

Botanist

Botanists are able to look at plant material recovered from a scene or body and give some clues about a plant's origin. They know which plants are indigenous to particular areas. This information may help in determining if a body was transported from one location to another.

Investigation and Autopsy

Investigation

Clues about the cause and manner of a death and who committed a crime may be found at a scene. Crime scene technicians, in addition to medical examiners, investigators, and law enforcement detectives, take part in examining a scene for clues. A crime scene technician meticulously inspects a scene and collects all necessary evidence. He is trained in discovering and preserving evidence for a criminalist and other experts to analyze. The following list includes different types of evidence and how they are usually collected and preserved.

Blood - Dried particles should be scraped into a dry container. Some dried areas may be sampled with a wet swab. A specimen should be dried before sealing it in a container. Articles of clothing or other objects containing blood may be submitted to a laboratory for sample removal by a technician.

Semen - An article of clothing containing semen should be collected or the specimen on the clothing can be lifted with water or saline.

Fingerprints - Soft objects that leave an impression may be collected in their entirety. Prints on hard objects like glass or furniture should be lifted at the scene.

Firearms and other weapons - These should be submitted to a lab without special treatment at a scene. A technician must ensure proper handling so that fingerprints are not smudged or ruined.

Bullets and cartridges- These should not be grasped with metal forceps because points of comparison may be damaged.

Hairs and fibers- These should be placed in separate containers and should not be crushed with hard objects such as metal tweezers.

Suspicious foods and pills - Each item should be placed in separate containers or bags to prevent contamination.

Footprints and tire marks- At the scene, casts should be made and close-up photographs should be taken.

Tool marks - There should be close-up photographs of the marks made by tools and, if possible, the damaged material should be removed for analysis by a lab technician.

Blood spatters - These should be photographed and described for analysis as to distance and angle of spatter. Samples may be removed for testing and preservation.

Other- Glass, soil, documents, cigarette butts, tobacco, and all items thought to be involved in arson should be collected and submitted to a lab.

Every scene should be diagrammed and photographed. Some jurisdictions are now using videotapes as well as photographs. Each item submitted to a lab should be referenced by either a photograph or written description as to its location in the scene. All containers with items submitted to the lab must be labeled on the lid and side of the container, with a case number, date, time, type of specimen, and name of the person who collected the specimen. A "chain of custody" begins at this point and continues until a disposition of the specimen is completed.

Scene investigation can be very useful in determining the approximate time of death. Different clues from a scene must not be overlooked: Was the mail picked up? Were the lights on or off? Was food being prepared? Was a major appliance on? Were there indicators as to a decedent's activities just prior to or at the time of death? A pathologist may use the answers to such questions to arrive at an estimation of the time of death, as discussed in Part II.

The Autopsy

The forensic pathologist conducts an autopsy. It is his responsibility to discover and describe all natural and traumatic disorders on a body. These findings should be described in an autopsy report which is completed after the examination. Injuries in suspicious cases and homicides should be photographed or videotaped. Information from a case must be retained in a decedent's case file for later review by any interested parties.

Cause of death is the most important piece of information obtained from an autopsy. The many causes of death and pathology of each are discussed in Part II. Besides documenting signs of injuries and natural diseases, a pathologist collects evidence which may be helpful in determining if a death was a homocide, suicide, natural, or an accident.

Some evidence which can be collected includes:

1. Blood - Blood is collected for drug screens, blood typing, and DNA comparisons. Blood for drug analyses can be collected in any container, but one containing fluoride oxalate prevents clotting and contamination from bacteria. Blood should be refrigerated and may even be frozen except if used for DNA testing and blood group typing. Dix's first rule of autopsies: "blood should be collected in every case because it's always better to have it and not use it than discover later that it was needed but never obtained."

2. Urine - Urine is good for screening drugs. If a urine screen is negative, blood usually does not have to be analyzed unless specific drugs not apparent on routine screening are suspected.

3. Anal, vaginal, and oral swabs - Cotton swabs are used to collect seminal fluid and sperm in suspected cases of rape. All swabs should be air dried prior to packaging.

4. Foreign material - Hair, thread, fragments of wood, metal, and any other foreign material should be collected in suspicious cases.

5. Clothing - Every article of clothing in homicides and suspicious cases should be dried and bagged. A pathologist should not cut clothing off a body in a suspected homicide. For example, if a pathologist cuts through the hole of an entry wound in a gunshot case, the hole will be distorted and future evaluation regarding point of entry or exit might be impossible. Local hospitals should retain clothing in traumatic cases until a

medical examiner or law enforcement official inspects them or gives permission for their disposal.

6. <u>Hair</u> - Scalp hair samples are routinely taken in homicides. Pubic hair samples are submitted if sexual assault is suspected and should be submitted separately. Hair samples should be taken from more than one site.

7. <u>Vitreous Humor</u> - This fluid is good for drug screens when urine is not available. It can also be used to quantitate ethyl alcohol, electrolytes (especially sodium and chloride), urea, creatinine, and glucose.

A pathologist may submit other fluids and organs from a body for drug testing as he deems necessary. Some labs prefer different tissues and fluids such as brain and bile. A pathologist usually knows a lab's preference. All evidence and specimens should be placed in separate containers and labeled as previously discussed to preserve chain of custody.

An autopsy includes complete exterior and interior examination of a body. A pathologist must perform a complete autopsy to determine cause of death. Certain cases may involve multiple causes of death such as ruptured aneurysms, heart disease, emboli, and trauma. Only a complete autopsy would reveal these multiple causes. Occasionally, a cause of death cannot be determined. Partial autopsies are not acceptable.

After an extensive external examination a pathologist usually begins an autopsy with a standard Y-shaped incision: the short arms of the Y are subclavicular and connected at just below the sternal notch; the long arm of the Y is virtually a straight line from sternal notch to symphysis pubis except at the umbilicus where care is taken to go slightly periumbilical. This retains the umbilicus for closure and gives the embalmer a point of reference. The skin is reflected exposing the chest and abdomen and the chest plate is removed. The organs are then removed either en-bloc (i.e., Rokitansky method) or individually (i.e., Virchow method). There is no one proper method. The objective is to find the cause of death. Of course, a prosector should be aware of the final disposition of the body, i.e., cremation or burial. An embalmer may have a difficult time if a pathologist makes many unnecessary incisions or cuts vessels too short which are needed for embalming.

A pathologist samples internal organs for microscopic examination when necessary. The cause of death is usually determined at the end of the gross examination. Microscopic analysis tends to shed little light on most cases, especially those in which trauma is the cause of death. If microscopic examination is performed, however, then a final diagnosis is not usually given until the slides are read. Some jurisdictions make slides on most cases while others do not. There is no rule as to how often or how many microscopic sections are taken.

A final autopsy report is generated when all data including toxicology have been analyzed. There should be an injury section separate from other external findings. Reviewing a disorganized report would obviously be difficult especially if different kinds of information were buried randomly in various sections. A list of final diagnoses and opinions or comments should also be separate from the main body of the report. There should be no editorializing or interpreting in the report, except in the opinion or comment section. A pathologist usually leaves interpretations or hypotheses to the trial or press conference.

Guidelines for the Death Scene Investigator
Mary Fran Ernst

In most jurisdictions, the body of a deceased individual and death scene are the responsibilities of a medical examiner's (or coroner's) office and the law enforcement agency, respectively. A medicolegal death investigator is a medical examiner's or coroner's representative. This person should be better trained and more knowledgeable of the cause and manner of death than any other investigator at the death scene. This death investigator should focus on the physical condition of a body at a scene. Preliminary scene information regarding injuries, trace evidence, identification, and estimation of time of death may be extremely useful to other specialists. Without a scene investigation by a trained investigator, much initial, valuable body information can be lost. The following 15 points will serve as a guide for death investigators.

1. Pre-plan the death investigation.
   When initially notified, a death investigator should determine as much information as possible from the caller. Approximate age and gender places a subject in a certain "medical category." Determining where a decedent has been found is helpful in investigational planning. An attempt should be made to ascertain if there is any evidence of foul play or if any instruments are available that might have played a role in the subject's death. By gathering these

data, a death investigator is able to anticipate additional information that may be needed upon arrival at a scene.

2. Establish telephone contact with the death scene.

If an investigator is notified by a law enforcement agency dispatcher or another individual who is not on the scene, he should attempt to contact a law enforcement official or other individual (funeral director, etc.) at the death scene. By speaking directly with one of these individuals, additional information can be gained which assists in planning necessary investigational scene activities. When speaking with this individual, a realistic expected arrival time should be provided.

3. Notification of personnel transporting the remains.

If possible, personnally speak to personnel who move a decedent to the morgue. Explain the nature of a decedent's condition so personnel can be prepared if special handling is required (e.g., decomposition, infection, etc). This information will be appreciated and will give the personnel additional time to prepare. The investigator is the best person to determine how much time before the body can be moved.

4. Cooperation among investigators.

A successful death investigation, involving more than one

individual, requires cooperation and coordination. Any potential conflicts should be worked out. Each office should have standard operating procedures which define the legal responsibilities for each investigating agency. Investigators from different agencies should meet prior to working actual cases so that potential areas of conflict can be discussed in an amicable and professional manner.

5. Photographs of decedent at death scene.
    Usually, a law enforcement agent takes photographs of a scene. This should be done prior to disturbing the scene or the deceased. Occasionally, a death investigator may also take photographs for a forensic pathologist performing the autopsy. Information such as body location and unique circumstances at the death scene may help a pathologist. It is important to keep in mind the legal implications of the photographs. Will the photographs be subpoenaed? Are they considered a part of the official medical examiner's inquiry? If a death investigator suspects a violent or suspicious death, a law enforcement agent should take the photographs.

6. Identification of the deceased.
    Positive identification of the decedent is crucial in all death inquiries. The family should be notified. Information such as medical history, work, and social history can only be obtained after an identification is established. Care must be

taken to insure that the identification is absolutely correct.

7. Examination of the body.

A systematic, thorough inspection and evaluation of the decedent should be performed by an investigator. If an investigator always begins at the top of a subject's body and moves toward the feet, the possibility of missing important injuries or evidence is lessened. Many inexperienced investigators focus on a major injury and neglect to evaluate the rest of the individual. This can lead to important oversights such as fingernail marks, bruises, and abrasions. Documentation of this inspection should be made noting the presence and absence of unusual markings or abnormalities. Descriptions of the state of rigor and livor mortis as well as the body temperature of a subject helps a forensic pathologist to estimate the time interval since death. Environmental assessment, including temperature, heating or cooling systems, moisture, and wind conditions must be made at a death scene so that the environmental influence on a decedent can be determined. The assessment should also include the types of clothing and jewelry. This information may be needed to assist in determinating the time a subject was last seen alive. Clothing should be appropriate for the weather and location found. If not, it needs to be explained. One should also determine if the clothing fits an individual. If a subject is decomposing, then clothing may appear too small due to body swelling. If the clothing is the incorrect size, one must determine why. Was the person wearing someone else's when death occurred? Or, was the decedent redressed by another person after death? Note the cleanliness of the clothing. A variance in the clothing or body cleanliness may indicate that he was handled by another individual after death. Is the clothing worn properly? Are buttons fastened and zippers closed? It is common to find opened zippers in intoxicated males or some elderly persons living alone. If the clothing is inconsistent with normal dressing techniques, consider whether a subject had a disability contributing to this behavior.

Jewelry should be carefully noted and reported as to its type, style, color and body location. All jewelry must be listed, regardless of its apparent value. Obvious "missing" jewelry should also be noted, such as only one pierced earring, or no wedding ring on a married individual. Currency and credit cards should be handled as valuable items. Currency should be counted in the presence of another and credit card details noted. If an investigator decides that these items may be given to the next-of-kin at the death scene, he must be certain that the relative has the legal right to such items.

No analyses should be performed on a decedent's body at a scene, such as gunshot residue or fingerprinting, without the expressed consent of the forensic pathologist responsible for the postmortem examination. Clothing should not be removed, a body should not be cleansed, and liquids or powders should not be placed on the deceased as these might interfere with radiographs or chemical testing. If more than one hour has elapsed since the initial body assessment and the decedent is still at the scene, a second assessment should be recorded. A thorough body visualization by an investigator gives him the capability to differentiate between injuries noted at a scene and any bodily injuries sustained during conveyance to the morgue.

8. Other scene information collection.

An investigator must also gather information that relates to cause and manner of death. Each type of death requires specific scene information. For instance, questions to be asked in a motor vehicle fatality would not be the same as those asked in an autoerotic asphyxial death. Since different questions need to be asked, an investigational guide for each specific type of death can be very useful. For example, it is critical in suicides resulting from a handgun that investigators determine the handedness of a subject. Several death investigation case guides are available in many jurisdictions.

9. Determine what information has already been developed.

Prior to an investigator's arrival, law enforcement officers, paramedics, and other support personnel probably have communicated with individuals or witnesses at the scene.

An investigator needs to know this initial information so that he can compare it with the decedent's body data and determine if there are any discrepancies. It is better to ask the question twice and get the same answer, than to accept as fact information that has been checked by one source. An investigator needs to determine, for instance, if the body data (rigor, livor, temperature, clothing, injuries, etc.) are different from the witness information.

10. Collect evidence items that may have contributed to the subject's death.

Any item that is on or attached to the decedent belongs to a medicolegal death investigator. Any item found at the scene, separate from a decedent, is under the control of the law enforcement agency. Any weapon or other item possibly related to the death and found at a scene should be brought to the morgue for analysis by a forensic pathologist. Often, substances are the causative agent in the death. All medication and alcoholic beverage containers should be confiscated as these will be invaluable to the toxicologists. Note the location where each item was found. Studies have shown that a fatal intoxicant is likely to be found in the same location as a decedent. Any drug paraphernalia, notes, or any unusual item that might have been used by the subject should be confiscated. In search and seizure of evidence, it is important that items needed for an investigator's evaluation be taken while he has control of the scene.

Investigators may not confiscate any items without the permission of the owner once control of the scene is lost to law enforcement officials.

11. Interviewing persons regarding the death.

A jurisdiction's standard operating procedure dictates who should be interviewed and by whom. Interviews should include basic information such as the subject's identification, clothing, time, date, state of health, date and time the body was discovered, and medical, employment, and social history. Any recent events that may have a bearing on the death are also important. A death investigator should always ask if a decedent had recently been involved in any potential harmful situations. This information may be extremely helpful if later attempts are made to make a prior incident a contributing factor in the death. If suicide is suspected, it is preferable to interview family members and close friends as soon as possible after the death is discovered. This may preclude guilt-related, subconscious, erroneous statements made by loved ones several days later.

12. Transporting the body.

A postmortem examination reveals all injuries present on a decedent. A decedent should not sustain additional injuries or be tampered with between the time the he is transported from a scene to the pathologist. An investigator may help alleviate potential problems by being present while transporting a subject from a scene to the morgue. Subjects can be protected by clean white sheets which should be brought to a scene by the death investigator or members of his office. To avoid any possible contamination with trace evidence at the scene, materials from a scene should not be used. Trace evidence on extremities and the head can be protected by using paper bags secured by tape. Careful attention should be paid to locating objects that might be loosely caught in a decedent's hair or clothing. After movement of a decedent by a conveyance team, an investigator should check to see if any item has been left behind. Professional and trustworthy personnel who transport the remains are crucial to the completion of the scene investigation. An investigator is responsible for a decedent and should be familiar with anyone who comes in contact with the body. Any problems regarding the careful and respectful handling of a subject or his valuables should be immediately controlled by an investigator.

13. Pronouncement of death.

A jurisdiction's law dictates who can perform this function. Many paramedical personnel will not pronounce an individual dead for fear of associated legal problems. A definite pronouncement date, place, and time is required for completion of a death certificate. This information should always be clearly stated in an investigator's death report.

Problems may arise when a subject is found in a

decomposed state, since death probably did not occur on the day that a body was discovered. Noting that the date of death is actually the "date of discovery" may solve this dilemma. Also, the problem of survivorship may occur when two persons (usually spouses) die as a result of the same incident. If possible, it is important to note, for insurance purposes, who expired first.

14. Family notification.

The most unpleasant task in a death investigation is notifying a family of a sudden, unexpected death. It is often an investigator's responsibility. Family reaction to this news is based upon: cultural norms, guilt, and a subject's place within the family structure. It is important that a family be notified of the death only when an investigator is certain of a victim's identification. If the identification is not solidly based on scientific evidence (e.g., dental exam, fingerprints, or radiographic comparison), then caution must be exercised in declaring a positive identification. When subjects are decomposed, thermally injured, or physically mutilated, an investigator should resist the temptation to accept personal papers or visual identification as the only sources. If a body is misidentified, two identification errors have been made: a suspected dead person may be alive, and a suspected living person is dead.

The media's job is to acquire information but an investigator should prevent further emotional harm to a decedent's family, or premature dissemination of valuable crime-solving information. It is wise to allow at least one hour after notifying the immediate family members of the sudden death before releasing any decedent's name to the press. It has been found that suicides are often mimicked, especially by young people. Common practice is not to discuss apparent suicides with the news media. The longer the media is deprived of that information, the less newsworthy it becomes.

15. The investigative report.

This document should contain information from each of the sections addressed above. The report should be in a form that can easily be understood by forensic professionals and laymen. If a death investigator wishes to be known as a professional, he needs to write like one. Correct grammar and spelling are mandatory. Reports should be written in chronological order. This protects an investigator from being accused of poor decision-making. If conflicting information is presented later, a death investigator can readjust the decision based on the new information. The report, however, must include all items that were part of the evaluation. This report will be utilized by many professionals within the department and from outside agencies. An investigator should carefully check his report before it is released since it reflects the competence of an investigator.

PART II
Forensic Pathology

Cause, Manner, And Mechanism Of Death

A forensic pathologist must determine how and why a person died by performing a thorough autopsy and studying the results of a good scene investigation. Both are essential in determining the correct cause, manner, and mechanism of death. The cause of death is the injury or disease which begins a sequence of events that ultimately leads to death. The cause of death may be either proximate or immediate, the initial and last events prior to death, respectively. For example, a beam falls on the back of a man working at a construction site leaving him paralyzed. As a result of paralysis he loses bladder control and becomes susceptible to urinary tract infections. Years after the accident he develops a severe kidney infection (pyelonephritis), becomes hospitalized, and ultimately dies. In this case, the proximate cause of death is the injury which left him paralyzed. The immediate cause is pyelonephritis. The length of time between a proximate and immediate cause does not change the ultimate cause of death as long as the sequence of events between the two is continuous. The time frame may be minutes, days, or years.

The mechanism of death is the biochemical or physiologic abnormality resulting in death. Examples of mechanisms of death are: shock, ventricular fibrillation or cardiorespiratory arrest. The mechanism of death is not the cause of death and should not appear alone on a death certificate. For example, someone who suffers a gunshot wound to the head, pulpification of the brain, and resultant cerebral edema (the mechanism of death) are not included on a certificate; the correct cause of death is a gunshot wound to the head (See figure 1). The manner of death is the circumstance surrounding a death. Traditionally, the manner is classified as one of the following: homicide, suicide, accident, natural, or undetermined. For example, if a man dies from sepsis as a result of a paralyzing injury, the manner of death is an accident.

Proximate Cause	Immediate Cause	Mechanism
Stab Wound	Pneumonia	Septicemia (Infection)
Gunshot Wound	Loss of Blood	Shock

Figure 1
Examples of Cause and Mechanism of Death

In order for a pathologist to determine the cause, manner, and mechanism of death, a complete investigation must be performed. An autopsy alone is not sufficient. Moreover, the circumstances of a death scene and a detailed history of the decedent are necessary.

Time Of Death, Decomposition, And Identification

Time of Death

Determination of the time of death, or the interval between the time of death and when a body is found (i.e., postmortem interval), can be difficult. A forensic pathologist attempts to determine the time of death as accurately as possible realizing, however, that such a determination is only a best estimate. Unless a death is witnessed, or a watch breaks during a traumatic incident, the exact time of death cannot be determined. The longer the time since death, the greater the chance for error in determining the postmortem interval. There are numerous individual observations which, when used together, provide the best estimate of the time of death. These include: rigor mortis, livor mortis, body temperature, decompositional changes, and stomach contents. A thorough scene investigation must also be performed and environmental conditions should be documented. The environment is the single most important factor in determining the postmortem interval.

Rigor Mortis

After death, the muscles of the body initially become flaccid. Within one to three hours they become increasingly rigid and the joints freeze by a process named rigor mortis (or postmortem rigidity or rigor). Although the exact chemical reaction causing muscles to stiffen has not been determined, rigor mortis is similar to physiologic muscle contraction and involves calcium, ATP, and ADP. The difference, however, is the formation of locking chemical bridges between the muscle proteins actin and myosin, and lack of muscle shortening in rigor mortis. In physiologic muscle contraction, actin molecules slide over myosin and the muscle shortens.[1]

Rigor mortis is affected by body temperature and metabolic rate: the higher the body temperature, more lactic acid is produced, and rigor occurs sooner. For example, a person dying with pneumonia and a fever will develop rigor sooner than a person with normal body temperature. Similarly, if a person's muscles were involved in strenuous physical activity just before death, rigor develops much more quickly. The process is also retarded in cooler environmental temperatures and accelerated in warmer ones.

All muscles of the body begin to stiffen at the same time after death. Muscle groups appear to stiffen at different rates because of their different sizes. For example, stiffness is apparent sooner in the jaw than in the knees. Thus, an examiner must check to see if joints are moveable in the jaws, arms, and legs.

A body is said to be in complete rigor when the jaw, elbow, and knee joints are immovable. This takes approximately 10-12 hours at an environmental temperature in the range of 70 - 75 °F. A body remains rigid for 24-36 hours before the muscles begin to loosen, apparently in the same order they stiffened.

A body remains rigid until rigor passes or a joint is physically moved and rigor is broken. Consequently, in addition to an estimate of the time of death, body position in full rigor can indicate whether or not a body has been moved after death.

Livor Mortis

Livor mortis is the discoloration of the body after death by the settling of blood no longer being pumped through the body by the heart. Blood settles in vessels by gravity in dependent areas of the body and colors the skin purple red. Some dependent areas may not discolor because skin compressess against a bony surface and prevents blood from settling in capillaries. For example, if blood settles to the back, pale areas occur over the scapula and buttocks. Livor mortis is noticeable approximately one hour after death. The color increases in intensity, becomes "fixed" in about 8 hours, does not blanche under pressure, and remains in those areas even if a body is repositioned. There may be a slight discoloration in new dependent areas after repositioning even though the blood remains fixed in the original position. Fixed blood seen in a nondependent location indicates that a body has been moved after death. Livor mortis is visible until the body becomes completely discolored by decomposition.

Variations in color during livor mortis depend on the cause of death. Carbon monoxide or cyanide poisoning, hypothermia, and refrigeration cause bright, cherry red livor mortis. People who die from extensive blood loss have very light or nonexistent livor mortis due to the small amount of blood in their system. Livor mortis is more difficult to determine in dark-skinned individuals. In some cases, capillaries in dependent areas rupture causing small hemorrhages or bleeds. These hemorrhages, called "Tardieu" spots, are particularly common in distal extremities of hanging victims. If they occur on the head they should not be mistaken for smaller pinpoint hemorrhages called petechiae. Petechiae occur when death is due to any sudden increase in blood pressure, such as a sudden stoppage of the heart in natural death, or in chest or neck compression in accidents or strangulation. They are commonly seen on the head, in the eyes, and internal organs.

Body Cooling (Algor mortis)

After death, the body cools from its normal internal temperature to the surrounding environmental temperature. Many studies have examined this decrease in body temperature to determine formulae which could predict its consistency. Unfortunately, because of numerous variables, body cooling is an inaccurate method of predicting postmortem interval. In general, however, evaluating a decrease in body temperature is most helpful within the first ten hours after death. During this time, with a normal body temperature and at an ideal environmental temperature of 70 - 75°F, the body cools at approximately 1.5°F per hour.

The problem with using the 1.5°F per hour calculation is the assumption that the internal and environmental temperatures are 98.6° and 70 - 75°, respectively. If a decedent's body temperature were higher than normal because of infection or physical exercise, 98.6° could not be used. Furthermore, the outside environment is rarely in the 70 - 75° range. For example, a body may actually gain heat if an individual expires outdoors in July, when temperatures may be greater than 100°. Conversely, if a person expires in a 25° environment, rapid cooling will take place.

Nonetheless, if body temperature is measured at a scene it should be taken on at least two separate occasions before a body is moved. A rectal or liver temperature is the most accurate measurement. The environmental temperature should also be recorded. If these relatively simple procedures are followed, a very crude estimate of the postmortem interval can be made.

Chemical Analyses

Various components in blood, cerebral spinal fluid, and vitreous humor have been studied as a means to determine time of death. Unfortunately, none of the studies have been conclusive. Vitreous potassium has received the most attention over the years, but its use has been limited because of individual case variation.

Gastric Contents

The total volume and description of food, liquid, or other

material present in the stomach should be recorded at autopsy. This information is helpful not only for identifying the composition of a decedent's last meal, but also for estimating the time of the last meal. For example, if a body was discovered in the evening, and only breakfast-type food was present in the gastric contents, this finding would suggest that death occurred in the morning. In addition, gastric emptying time can be useful if taken in context with other information. In general, a light meal takes approximately two hours to pass through the stomach while a heavy meal might take up to six hours. Some foods such as celery or tomato skins take longer than meat or other vegetables to pass through the stomach to the duodenum. The rate of digestion is also dependent upon the mental and physical state of the victim prior to death. An excited person, threatened with violence, may have either a slower or quicker than normal gastric emptying time.

Scene Investigation

Clues about the time of death may also be found at a scene either away from, near to, or on the body. Evidence such as the type of insects on the body, flora beneath the body, or objects from a decedent's residence may be contributing clues.

Insect larvae on the body can be collected and saved in alcohol. An entomologist will be able to state not only the type of larvae, but also their developmental stage. Each stage has a specific time duration which enables an entomologist to state how long the larvae have been present on a body. It does not represent a postmortem interval because a body may have been dead for a period of time prior to insect infestation.

Flora discovered under or near a body may be helpful. A botanist would be needed to examine the specimen, classify the type of flora according to time of year normally present, and determine how much time elapsed to reach that particular growth stage. Use of entomological and botanical data may narrow the time of death to weeks or months, but rarely days.

Information from a scene not associated with a body may also be critical in estimating the time of death. All clues from a house or an apartment, for example, must be analyzed circumspectly. Was the mail picked up? Were the lights on? Was food being prepared? Was a major appliance on? Was there any indication as to activities an individual was performing, had completed, or was contemplating? How was the person dressed? The best estimate of time of death can be made by utilizing all available information from a scene and performing a careful external and internal examination of a body.

Decomposition

In general, as rigor passes, skin first turns green in the abdomen. As discoloration spreads to the rest of the trunk, the body begins to swell due to bacterial methane gas formation. These bacteria are normal inhabitants of the body. They proliferate after death and their overgrowth is promoted in warm weather and retarded in cold weather.

The different rates and types of decomposition a body undergoes depends upon the environment. Bodies buried in earth, submerged in water, left in the hot sun, or placed in a cool basement, appear different after the same postmortem interval. When a body is bloated, epidermal sloughing and hemoglobin degradation begin. Degenerated blood stains blood vessels causing subcutaneous ones to become visible through the skin. This pattern is called "subcutaneous marbling." Moreover, as bloating continues, hair is forced from the skin. The increased internal pressure, caused by bacterial gas production, forces decomposed blood and body fluids out of body orifices by a process called "purging." As the body undergoes skeletonization, the rate of tissue deterioration is dependant on environmental temperature. For example, a body exposed to a 100° environmental temperature may completely decompose to a skeleton within a few weeks. In contrast, a body at 65° may not skeletonize for many months or years. In general, a body decomposing above ground for a week looks similar to a body that has been under water for two weeks or one buried for six weeks. This generalization should serve as a reminder that an uncovered or naked body decomposes more rapidly than a covered or clothed one.

After a body is found, it is usually refrigerated until an autopsy is performed or a final disposition is made. Decomposition slows down or ceases if a body is refrigerated. When re-exposed to room temperature decomposition occurs rapidly. Recognition of this accelerated decomposition is particularly important if a person dies in a cold environment and is then moved to a warmer one.

Decomposition may be asymmetric. For example, decomposition occurs more rapidly in injured areas. If a man is struck on the head, and bleeding occurs only in that area, decomposition may be much more advanced on the head than on the remainder of the body. Fly larvae proliferate during summer, spring, and fall in warm, moist areas of the body such as the eyes, nose, and mouth. Larvae are attracted to injured areas where they feed on exposed blood proteins and cause accelerated decomposition. Due to asymmetric decomposition, it is common to see skeletonization in only one part of the body.

Adipocere

Adipocere is a term derived from Latin which literally means "fat" (adipo) "wax"(cera). It refers to a waxy substance formed during decomposition.[2] It is an uncommon change occurring particularly in bodies buried in moist environments and is characteristically seen after bodies have been submerged in water during the winter months. Fatty tissue beneath the skin begins to saponify. This hardening, which takes a minimum of a few weeks to develop, keeps a body in a relatively preserved state for many months or years. Unlike normal decompositional changes, there is no green discoloration or significant bloating. The bacteria which normally proliferate and form gas are inhibited by cold temperatures. The body's exterior remains white and the outermost layers of the skin slip off.

For bodies totally submerged in water, adipocere will be evenly distributed over all surfaces. Not all bodies having adipocere are found in water. For example, bodies found in bags, which provide a moist environment, may also undergo this change. In this situation there may be a differential development of adipocere depending on whether or not areas of the body are clothed.

Mummification

Mummification occurs in hot, dry environments. The body dehydrates and bacterial proliferation is minimal. The skin becomes dark, dried, and leathery. The process occurs readily in the fingers and toes in dry environments regardless of the temperature. Most mummified bodies are found in summer months. It is also common for this process to occur in winter months if the environment is warm. An entire body can mummify in a few days to weeks. As the skin begins to dry and harden, soft tissues beneath the skin begin to decompose. After a few weeks, an entire body may appear preserved with some shrinkage due to dehydration. If an incision is made through the skin, however, soft tissues, fat, and internal organs may be virtually absent with the body resembling a "bag of bones." Once a body is in this state, it may remain preserved for many years unless the skin is torn or broken.

Identification

The most important question to answer in any death is the identification of a decedent. An individual will not be charged with a crime or a family will not collect on an insurance policy if the identity of a decedent is unknown. In non-forensic deaths, identifying the remains is rarely a concern because most people die at home or in a hospital. Identification is often in question in forensic cases because of one of the following: death commonly occurs away from home and next of kin may not be readily available to view a body, a person dies alone, or a family is unable to identify the remains.

A decedent is often positively identified. Occasionally this cannot be accomplished and a presumptive identification must be made. There are a number of ways a decedent can be identified. Positive identification can be made visually and by fingerprints, teeth, x-rays, and DNA testing ("fingerprinting"). Presumptive identification can be made by bones, clothing, x-ray, other physical characteristics, and circumstances surrounding a death.

Positive identification
Visual

Most identifications are made visually. Family members are notified of a death and may go to a funeral home, morgue, or hospital to make an identification. This may be quite unpleasant for a family. Some jurisdictions require next of kin to make an identification in person; others will attempt to alleviate some of the emotion by allowing a family member to view a photograph of the face or body. Some jurisdictions suggest that relatives not look at a body until after it has been prepared for viewing at a funeral home. A viewing at a morgue is only a formality. Authorities may have a driver's license or some other form of identification and are certain that the decedent is the person in question.

Even though this method of identification is the most common and easiest, problems may be encountered. Numerous injuries may disfigure a body making identification difficult. A body may undergo decomposition, which may dramatically alter a body because of skin slippage, bloating, and discoloration. A young white man, for example, may have so much skin discoloration and bloating with skin slippage that he may appear to be an older black man. Hair, mustaches, and beards may slip off the skin. These changes may keep a family from making positive identification. They may be in denial about a relative's death and use any change in appearance to support the possibility that death did not occur.

Fingerprints

The second most common means of identification is through the use of fingerprints. Approximately 200 million people have their fingerprints on file with law enforcement or other agencies. Since the science of fingerprinting has advanced significantly over the last fifty years, mistakes rarely occur.

Technological advances have helped agencies store fingerprint data, thereby shortening the time it takes to match unknowns to knowns.

Dental

Unless a decedent is edentulous, dental comparison is an excellent method for making a positive identification. A forensic pathologist or an odontologist can make the comparison but difficult cases should be analyzed by the latter. Many forensic pathologists prefer not to make these comparisons and turn all dental exams over to the odontologist.

Often decedents with a complete set of dentures can be identified. A technician who made the dentures may put the decedent's name or some other form of personal identification on the denture, or he may recognize his work even without some form of identification.

X-rays

Many individuals have had x-rays taken. These antemortem studies can be used for postmortem comparisons made by either radiologists or forensic pathologists. A radiologist should be consulted if the case is difficult. Although a chest film is often used for comparison, it is not as good as a skull or pelvis film and more difficult to match with an unknown. The pelvis and skull have more points of bony variations than the chest making them easier to match.

DNA fingerprinting

All individuals except identical twins have unique DNA. "DNA fingerprint" is a common term used to imply that our genetic composition (i.e., our DNA) is similar to our inked fingerprint. Please see Part III, "DNA Testing" for further information.

Presumptive identification

Skeletal remains

Skeletal remains are usually examined by an anthropologist, preferably a forensic anthropologist. Forensic anthropologists are experts in estimating age, gender, and race, and may use numerous scientific formulae to arrive at their conclusions. Age estimations are the most difficult and are determined by microscopic analysis. A thin slice of bone is placed under a microscope and structures called osteons are counted. The number of osteons in a given area provides an estimated age. Even with the help of this procedure an anthropologist cannot make a positive identification. A presumptive identification can be made if a skeleton fits the description of a missing person or, some form of personal identification, such as a driver's license, is discovered with a body and the skeletal characteristics match height, race, and gender on the license.

Clothing

The style, size, and manufacturer of clothing are commonly used to make a presumptive identification. Relatives or friends may remember what a missing person was last wearing. Unfortunately, many clothes decompose with a body or are destroyed if a body is burned.

X-rays

Antemortem x-rays do not ensure a positive identification. There may not be enough points of variation allowing a radiologist to render a conclusive opinion. A presumptive identification may be made if the x-rays are consistent with those of the decedent and there is no reason to suspect a person to be someone else.

Physical features

Tattoos, scars, birthmarks, the absence of organs from surgical procedures, and other physical anomalies are helpful in making identifications. The presence or absence of any of these characteristics may also be helpful in eliminating any possible matches, or in making a possible identification.

Circumstances surrounding death

Identifications may be impossible to make based on a few remains discovered at a scene. The circumstances in which the remains are discovered, however, may allow an identification to be made. For example, if only a few pieces of a body are located in a burned home, an identification cannot be made based on scientific testing. If the owner was last seen in the house, or if there is no other reason to believe the remains are those of someone else, a presumptive identification of the owner can still be made.

References:

1. Perper JA: Time of death and changes after death. Part 1. Anatomical Considerations. In Spitz WU (ed.): Spitz and Fisher's Medicolegal Investigation of Death: Guidelines for the Application of Pathology to Crime Investigation, 3rd ed. Springfield: Charles C. Thomas, 1993, pp.26-27.
2. Dorland's Illustrated Medical Dictionary, 28th ed. Philadelphia: W.B. Saunders, Co., 1994.

Sudden Natural Death

A medical examiner is not concerned with all natural deaths. His job is to investigate those that are unwitnessed or might be considered suspicious. A history determines whether death is sudden and unexpected, or expected. Many people who die suddenly have long histories of chronic natural disease. Medical examiners are not concerned with such cases. Most autopsy cases are traumatic deaths. Autopsies are usually not necessary when an investigation reveals that a decedent suffered from a chronic disease or a body is discovered under non-suspect conditions.

Cardiovascular Disease
Arteriosclerotic Heart Disease

Besides being the leading cause of death, cardiovascular disease is also the leading cause of sudden unexpected natural death. Arteriosclerosis (literally "hardening" of the arteries) refers to a group of disorders that have in common thickening and loss of elasticity of arterial walls.[1] Atherosclerosis, characterized by intimal thickening and lipid deposition, is one such disease and the most common. Atherosclerosis primarily affects elastic arteries, such as the aorta, carotids and iliacs, as well as large and medium sized muscular arteries, such as the coronaries. Cardiac arrhythmia is the main complication of atherosclerotic coronary artery disease. It is also the final event of many kinds of natural disease. A cardiac arrhythmia cannot be detected by either gross or microscopic examination of the heart. Consequently, it is a mechanism of death which is determined by excluding all other possibilities.

A medical examiner who views an elderly person dead in bed without signs of foul play will probably determine the cause of death to be secondary to arteriosclerotic disease and will not perform an autopsy. This diagnosis is the most common in apparent natural deaths, whether or not an autopsy is performed. Since the disease is so prevalent, it is probably overused as a cause of death when no autopsy is performed.

Atherosclerotic coronary artery disease is also the most common cause of acute and chronic ischemic heart disease. In both types of ischemia, proper oxygenation of the myocardium is prevented due to inadequate blood flow. In acute ischemic heart disease, the decrease in blood flow is due to sudden obstruction of an artery by a thrombus. In chronic ischemic heart disease, there is a gradual narrowing of the vessel's lumen due to a build up of atherosclerotic plaque. Arrhythmia is also the most common mechanism of sudden unexpected death in atherosclerotic coronary artery disease.

At autopsy, the degree of coronary artery obstruction which has produced death is often quite variable. The amount of obstruction needed to cause death varies between individuals and circumstances. A man with known severe triple coronary artery disease may live for many years while one with only moderate single vessel disease may die suddenly without having any previous signs or symptoms.

Hypertensive Heart Disease

An enlarged heart with no other significant pathology is usually regarded as a hypertensive heart. In many instances, however, there will be no history of high blood pressure.

Sudden death in people with hypertensive heart disease may be due to an arrhythmia or one of the other complications of hypertensive cardiovascular disease, such as a ruptured aorta or brain hemorrhage.

Other types of heart disease

Less common forms of heart disease which cause sudden death include congenital and valvular heart disease, cardiomyopathy, and myocarditis. There are numerous congenital abnormalities of the heart which may cause sudden death. Single coronary arteries and abnormal anatomic distributions of the coronaries are relatively common. Many severe problems, such as tetralogy of Fallot, are discovered at birth or shortly thereafter. Some people, however, may expire without a previous diagnosis. Valvular stenoses or dilatations, such as complications of rheumatic disease and mitral valve prolapse, are also common. Cardiomyopathies, such as asymmetrical hypertrophy of the heart and dilated idiopathic cardiomyopathy, may cause sudden death at a young age often during exercise. Sudden unexpected death from myocarditis may follow a flu-like illness.

Vascular Disease

In addition to atherosclerotic coronary artery disease there are a number of vascular diseases which cause sudden death. In most cases death does not occur as rapidly as it does when there is a sudden cardiac arrhythmia. The following list are some of the more common vascular diseases which cause sudden, unexpected death.

1. Ruptured cerebral aneurysm - Berry aneurysms, or saccular or congenital aneurysms, are the most frequent type of intracranial aneurysms. Rupture of these aneurysms may cause sudden death without prior warning symptoms. They are more common in the circle of Willis, especially in the area of the anterior and posterior communicating arteries. People rarely survive a ruptured berry aneurysm. A rupture may occur at a time of stress, during a sudden increase in blood pressure, or during a nonstressful occasion. A ruptured vessel may also be discovered at autopsy in an individual who has fallen and received other fatal injuries. In this unusual circumstance, the rupture precedes the fall and is not caused by the fall.

   At autopsy, hemorrhage is generally confined to the subarachnoid space but may occasionally extend into the subdural space. Hemorrhage is plentiful around the site of rupture at the base of the brain and spreads within the subdural space over the cerebral convexities. Microscopic sections of an aneurysm may be examined for signs of previous leakage. The presence of hemosiderin in surrounding tissues suggests that some leakage occurred prior to the fatal rupture.

2. Pulmonary thromboemboli - The vast majority of emboli originate in the deep veins of the lower extremities. They may also arise in pelvic veins, especially during pregnancy, or in extremities at the site of a previous injury. Thromboemboli most commonly develop in individuals who become bedridden after surgical procedures and in anyone whose activity level suddenly decreases.

Thromboemboli also occur in people with coagulation disorders such as protein S or C deficiency.

Since the lungs have a dual blood supply, the number and size of emboli that cause death are significant. Emboli that frequently cause sudden death tend to be found between the right and left pulmonary arteries forming a so-called "saddle embolus." Most emboli which cause sudden death are not adherent to a vessel wall. In order to diagnose a death from pulmonary emboli it is important to distinguish between thrombi formed prior to death and postmortem clots. Microscopic examination may be helpful in making this determination.

3. Ruptured aortic aneurysms - The statistics for untreated aortic aneurysms are grim. It is known, for instance, that abdominal aneurysms greater than 7 cm have a mortality between 72 and 83% if simply followed without surgical intervention.[2] Consequently, all aneurysms 5-6 cm in diameter should be corrected soon after diagnosis. They may or may not be symptomatic prior to rupture. A typical scenario is sudden cardiovascular collapse of an individual from a ruptured aortic aneurysm while being admitted to a hospital for acute abdominal pain. These aneurysms are caused by weakening of a blood vessel by atherosclerosis.

4. Acute aortic dissection - Acute aortic dissection is associated with hypertension or congenital connective tissue disorders, such as Marfan's syndrome, which can affect the aorta. A dissection often begins in an atherosclerotic plaque where bleeding into a vessel wall causes separation between layers of the aortic wall with tearing and ultimate rupture. There is

usually considerable pain with this disorder and rupture is often fatal unless the dissection occurs close to, or in, a hospital where care can be provided immediately. Recently, aortic dissections have been seen in cocaine abusers, presumably due to the rapid rise in blood pressure caused by the drug. In this situation, death is not due to natural causes and should be ruled an accidental complication of cocaine abuse.

Chronic Alcoholism

Chronic alcoholics may die suddenly, presumably from an arrhythmia. They may also have dilated cardiomyopathy due to the toxic effects of alcohol. The liver commonly contains fat and there may be alcohol in the blood. Death due to chronic alcoholism is considered natural. Death from acute alcohol intoxication, however, with a markedly elevated blood alcohol concentration, is considered accidental.

Central Nervous System (CNS) Disorders

Very few disorders of the CNS cause sudden and unexpected death. For example, brain tumors can cause sudden death, but patients usually present to a physician with signs and symptoms of their disease prior to death. Occasionally, a child dies suddenly from an unsuspected and undiagnosed rapidly growing tumor such as a cystic astrocytoma of the cerebellum. Colloid cysts of the third ventricle may also cause a sudden unexpected death. Meningitis may present with nonspecific symptoms, such as a headache, and may not be diagnosed in an emergency room. Within hours, the symptoms may progress rapidly and cause death before adequate medical attention is obtained.

The most common disorder of the CNS which causes a sudden death is a seizure. Seizures may be acquired or idiopathic. If the decedent developed a seizure disorder as a result of blunt trauma to the head, death is not considered natural because the cause of death was the result of trauma. Example of acquired seizures from natural causes are alcoholism and tumors. Seizures acquired from physiologic and metabolic abnormalities are the mechanism of death. It is important to recognize that the correct cause of death is the underlying disorder, not the seizure. Finally, there is a group of patients who have seizures without an underlying cause. These deaths are signed out as "idiopathic seizure disorder."

Identification of a gross or microscopic abnormality in the brain which triggers a seizure is rarely found. Clearly, a decedent's history and a complete drug screen are important when making a diagnosis of death due to seizures.

Respiratory Disorders

Sudden and unexpected deaths from respiratory disorders are usually due to infections. Infants may succumb to bronchopneumonia very suddenly and without exhibiting significant symptoms. Viral infections of the tracheobronchial tree may become secondarily infected by bacteria. An immunocompromised individual with AIDS or cancer readily develops respiratory infections, but these expected deaths are usually due to a chronic condition. In some areas, undiagnosed tuberculosis and other contagious diseases not associated with the immunocompromised host still cause unexpected deaths.

The Negative Autopsy

At least 1-2% of the deaths in a busy forensic jurisdiction will be undetermined and have negative autopsies. Such decedents tend to be younger individuals without previous injuries or medical problems. What does a pathologist do next? First, he makes sure a complete scene investigation is performed and reviews all autopsy findings and toxicology. If all this is unrewarding, most medical examiners believe these sudden unexplained deaths are due to arrhythmias, and are therefore natural. An appropriate cause of death in these cases is "arrhythmia due to an unknown cause or natural disorder." These deaths are not the same as sudden infant deaths which will be discussed in the pediatric section.

References:

1. Schoen FJ: Blood Vessels. In Cotran RS, Kumar V, Robbins SL (eds.): Robbins Pathologic Basis of Disease, 5th ed. Philadelphia, W.B. Saunders Co, 1994, p. 473.

2. Sabiston DC, Jr: Aortic Abdominal Aneurysms. In Sabiston DC, Jr (ed.): Textbook of Surgery: The Biological Basis of Modern Surgical Practice, 14th ed. Philadelphia, W.B. Saunders Co, 1991, p. 1567.

Firearms

Range and direction of gunshot wounds are important determinations to make in order to properly evaluate a firearms injury case. Interpretation of the range of fire is made by evaluating the presence or absence of gunpowder on skin and/or clothing. Direction of fire is determined by following the path of a bullet from an entrance to an exit wound or to the location of a bullet within a body.

Handguns and rifles fire ammunition or cartridges composed of a primer, gunpowder or propellant, and a bullet or projectile. Ammunition is remarkably similar for both except when used in the military or with other specific types such as specially coated bullets or exploding rounds. The primer is composed of elemental compounds such as antimony, barium, and lead in varying proportions. When a firing pin of a weapon strikes the primer, the resulting explosion ignites the gunpowder.

Gas pressure from the combustion of gunpowder in a confined space of a cartridge and gun barrel propels a bullet out of a muzzle. Gunpowder is usually composed of small flakes, spheres, or cylinders of nitroglycerine or nitrocellulose mixtures. Unburned and burning gunpowder particles may be discharged with a bullet. Gunpowder, vaporized primer, and metal from a gun may be deposited on skin and/or clothing of a victim. In addition, elements from the primer may be deposited on objects in close proximity to a discharged weapon.

The presence or absence of these primer elements can be

detected with a gunpowder residue test designed to aid in determining whether a particular individual has recently fired a gun. When a residue of completely burned gunpowder is deposited on skin, it produces an area of soot deposition referred to as "fouling." Gunpowder particles cause tattooing or stippling because they abrade or become embedded in skin and cannot be removed. Fouling or soot can be easily washed-off.

The most commonly used ammunition includes a bullet with a lead core that may or may not be covered with a copper jacket. Bullets may have flattened, rounded, or hollowed tips. Some handgun ammunitions contain numerous small pellets instead of containing one bullet. This is commonly called "birdshot" or "snakeshot."

The caliber of a handgun or rifle refers to the inside diameter of the barrel. The measurement is given in fractions of inches or millimeters. A .38 caliber handgun, for example, is 38/100 of an inch in diameter and would fire a .38 caliber bullet. Unfortunately, this system is not consistent. A .357 caliber handgun can fire the same size bullet as a .38, the difference being a greater amount of powder, giving the .357 a greater velocity and more destructive power. Inconsistencies in nomenclature are especially common with rifles. A barrel of a rifle or pistol has spiral grooves cast along its entire length, causing a bullet to pursue a tighter, straighter path once it exits a muzzle. Alternating grooves with uncut metal are called lands-and grooves. These lands-and-grooves make distinct impressions (or rifling marks) on bullets as they pass through a barrel. Different weapons have different patterns of lands-and-grooves and each weapon gives a unique characteristic wear pattern. Comparing the marks and wear patterns on a bullet recovered at autopsy with the pattern on a test fired bullet can make a positive identification of a murder weapon.

Range of Fire

Presence or absence of gunpowder residue on or in a target area indicates whether a range of fire was contact, loose, close, intermediate, or distant.

Tight contact - a muzzle of a weapon is held tightly against skin. All gunpowder residue is on the edges or in the depths of a wound. There may be searing or burning of wound margins or reddening of surrounding skin due to carbon monoxide gas produced by burning powder. In a tight contact wound to the head, there is often tearing of skin around the entrance wound because of a tremendous pressure buildup and blowback of skin toward a muzzle.

Loose contact - If a weapon is not held firmly against the skin, gunpowder may escape from a barrel and be deposited around the edges of a wound.

Close range - Close range gunshot wounds occur at muzzle-to-target distances up to 6 to 10 inches. Both fouling and stippling are found on clothing or skin. Microscopic examination discloses carbon debris (fouling) and possible partially burned flakes of gunpowder in the superficial and deeper layers of the skin.

Intermediate range - These wounds occur at muzzle-to-target distances of approximately 6 inches to 3 feet. There is no fouling, only stippling or deposition of particles on clothing.

Distant wounds - Distant wounds have neither fouling nor stippling on a target and do not have appreciable quantities of powder residue in a wound tract. Microscopic examination of distant wounds, however, can disclose a few particles of powder residue in a wound track. This would be likely if the ammunition contains ball powder, which can travel much further than flake powder.

In order to determine the exact distance of a weapon from a body, the same gun that caused the wound must be test fired with the same ammunition. The patterns are then compared with those seen on the decedent. If a suspected weapon is not recovered, a distance may only be estimated. If a bullet is recovered, however, estimates are usually quite accurate because ballistics experts can examine a bullet and give a knowledgeable determination of the weapon used.

Entrance and exit wounds are generally easy to differentiate. Entrance wounds tend to be circular defects with a thin rim of abrasion caused by a bullet scraping and perforating skin. Entrance wounds of the face can be quite atypical because the surfaces are not flat. A gunshot wound to the eye may not look like a gunshot wound because the eyelid may close over the defect. As previously mentioned, contact wounds of the skull might have multiple tears because of blowback of the skin against a muzzle.

Exit wounds may be circular like entrance wounds, but they are often irregular in shape. They may be slit-like or have ragged edges. They do not have a rim of abrasion like entrance wounds unless a victim's skin is pressed against another object. This is called a "shored" exit wound because there is a wide rim of abrasion. For example, if a man was shot while sitting in the front seat of his car and a bullet exits his back, the skin will be forced against the car seat causing an abrasion. This will happen whether or not a victim is wearing a shirt.

Skin around an exit wound may be discolored because of underlying bleeding in the soft tissues. Entrance wounds rarely have this surrounding contusion unless they are re-entry wounds. These wounds have more irregular shapes and abrasions than a typical circular entrance wound caused by a nondeformed and non-tumbling re-entry bullet.

Shotguns

Shotguns have smooth bores with no lands-and-grooves. This means that a particular weapon cannot be matched to pellets recovered at a scene or from a body. Range of fire is determined similarly to the way it is for handguns and rifles except that the degree of pellet spread can be more helpful.

Shotguns usually fire pellets, but they can also fire slugs. These solid projectiles are similar to large bullets except that they do not travel as far and usually stop in a target. They are commonly seen in some states which outlaw hunting deer with rifles.

Shotguns are designated by the diameter of the barrel, or bore. The unit of measure is the gauge. Shotgun gauge is determined in a unique way. Bore size is equal to the number of lead balls of similar diameter weighing one pound. A 12-gauge shotgun, for instance, has a barrel diameter that is the same circumference as 12 lead balls of similar diameter weighing a pound. A 16-gauge has a smaller diameter than a 12-gauge because 16 balls of an equal diameter that is less than the 12 would weigh one pound. The exception to this is the 410- gauge which is .410 inch in diameter.

Cutting and Stabbing

Cutting and stabbing injuries are second to firearms as the leading cause of homicides. They rarely present a pathologist with a diagnostic dilemma. Occasionally a blunt impact injury might appear similar to a cutting injury. Thorough external and internal examinations, however, would resolve any difficulties. A tear from blunt trauma tends to have ragged edges with tissue bridges extending across a wound. There may also be abrasions or contusions around wound margins. A cutting or incised wound does not have tissue bridges and its edges are rarely ragged.

Cutting (incised) wounds

An incised wound (cut) is made by a sharp instrument and

is longer on the skin surface than its depth. The edges of the wound are sharp and are usually not ragged or abraded. The surrounding skin is usually undamaged. Within the wound, tissue bridges do not connect one side to the other, as seen in a laceration. Virtually any sharp object may cause an incised wound.

Stab wounds

A stab wound is produced by a sharp object and causes a wound that is deeper than it is wide. The size of a skin defect rarely gives an indication of the depth of a stab wound. Depending on the weapon, the angles of an external wound may be sharp or blunt.

A single-edged pocket knife, for example, causes a defect having one blunt angle and one sharp angle. Double-bladed knives cause two sharp angles. Home-made sharpened weapons may produce unusual looking injuries having either sharp or dull angles. These types of weapons are commonly made by prisoners.

Most stab wounds are caused by knives, but any object with a sharp point can be used. Other common sharp weapons are screwdrivers, scissors, and ice picks. The general characteristics of an instrument causing a stab wound determine the entrance defect on the skin surface, the depth and size of the wound track, and the injuries to internal organs. In addition, portions of the instrument may break off and may be recovered in the wound track. Care must be taken when relating the size of an entrance wound on the skin surface to the dimensions of a weapon because the skin's elasticity (and Langer's lines) can stretch and distort a wound. The same weapon can cause apparently different injuries because of their different locations and orientations on the body. For example, the same angle of entry in both the chest and abdomen may cause a horizontal defect in the abdomen and a diagonal wound in the chest. A pathologist must carefully approximate the margins of the wound prior to determining the type of weapon. Occasionally, he cuts out the wound and saves it in formalin. This rarely helps because of tissue shrinkage.

The width and length of a weapon's blade may be determined by analyzing a stab wound. A 1/2-inch wide blade, for example, causes a 1/2-inch wide wound on the skin surface if a knife is inserted and removed straight. If either the victim or assailant moves, the external wound may be longer. An external wound may also be slightly shorter because of the skin's elasticity. If, for example, a 4-inch long blade is used, the depth of the wound track may be longer than the length of the blade because skin and surrounding tissues will collapse and spring back as the pressure is relieved. Similarly, the depth may be the same or shorter than the blade length.

Insight into the manner of death may be gained by observing the location(s) and type(s) of wounds. Multiple incised and/or stab wounds of the neck, face, and extremities (so-called "defense" wounds) are usually caused by an assailant. Multiple incised wounds of varying depths on the neck or wrists suggest a suicide. Superficially incised wounds adjacent to a major incised wound are referred to as hesitation marks and are characteristic of self-inflicted injuries. A body sustaining tens or hundreds of stab and incised wounds is characteristic of a situation known as overkill and usually occurs in a highly emotional setting such as one involving sex or drugs.

The length of time a person survives after receiving a fatal injury is at best an inexact determination unless the injury caused instantaneous death. Severely injured individuals may carry on seemingly impossible activities. For example, victims with stab wounds to the heart have run blocks or driven miles before they have collapsed.

An estimate of survival time can be based on the amount of blood lost internally and externally at the scene. A person can lose over a third of his blood volume before progressing to irreversible hemorrhagic shock. Of course, the amount of blood loss necessary to cause death is quite variable and depends on how fast the blood is lost and a decedent's general state of health. A person who is elderly or frail has little reserve to withstand blood loss. For example, a chronically ill individual may succumb after a 10-15% slow blood loss, while a healthy individual may lose 25% rapidly with few complications.

The amount of blood at a scene must be considered when determining total blood loss. It is impossible to predict the amount of blood from an examination of a wound or body. A wound in one individual might bleed profusely while a similar wound in another individual may not. It is difficult to determine an exact amount of blood at a scene. The amount of blood in a body cavity during an autopsy is easier to measure than attempting to estimate an amount at a scene. For example, a few hundred milliliters spread throughout a room can appear as if liters of blood were lost.

Pathologists may be asked to evaluate a decedent's degree of debilitation prior to death. Attorneys are interested in answers to these questions because they want to know what a decedent might have done, either aggressively or defensively, prior to death. This determination is also difficult and depends in part on the location of a wound. A stab wound to the spinal cord, for example, is one of the easiest to evaluate because the levels of motor and sensory control are well known. Questions about the degree of debilitation must be answered honestly and conservatively as individual variation in response to injuries is great. A pathologist must know his limitations when answering such questions.

Drugs And Alcohol

Most large medical examiner or coroner offices have their own toxicology labs dedicated almost exclusively to postmortem analyses, although some perform tests on street drugs. An office with its own lab is more likely to perform routine drug screens than those offices which send specimens to an outside toxicology lab. Pathologists in underfunded jurisdictions are forced to become selective in ordering tests. Ideally, a complete drug screen should be performed in all cases, or at least in every traumatic death. For example, a forty-year-old man who dies suddenly at work may appear to have died as the result of a heart attack. If he tests positive for cocaine, however, then cocaine would be a contributing cause. The manner of death would then be ruled an accident and not a natural one.

Almost any drug or chemical can cause death. Drugs are not the cause of death, however, in most medical examiner cases. Rather, drugs are present in many suicidal, homicidal, and accidental traumatic deaths. An accurate determination of the relationship of a drug to cause of death depends on the quality of a toxicology laboratory, autopsy findings, and scene investigation.

Most cases of an apparent drug overdose are straightforward. The circumstances and individual's history usually suggest a drug-related death. If there is no history, an autopsy will reveal signs of drug abuse such as needle punctures, track marks, and scars from skin popping. A poorly nourished or unkempt body habitus would also suggest drug involvement. An internal examination generally reveals nonspecific changes such as vascular congestion of organs and pulmonary edema without other causes of death.

Numerous textbooks list therapeutic and toxic concentrations of drugs and poisons.[1] These concentrations, however, are only a guideline for a forensic pathologist and should be used in conjunction with the circumstances of death. People have different tolerances to drugs based upon differences in absorption and metabolism. For example, drug addicts and alcoholics can usually tolerate higher drug levels than nonusers. There are many individuals who die by other means even though they have toxic concentrations of drugs and chemicals in their system.

Ethyl Alcohol

Ethanol is the most commonly abused drug in this country. Not only do thousands of alcoholics die from alcohol-induced diseases each year, but thousands die from trauma caused either by themselves or someone else when intoxicated. Alcohol is a factor in a large number of homicides and traffic fatalities.

The legal limit to be considered driving under the influence of alcohol in most states is 100 mg % or .10 grams %. This is an equivalent amount of alcohol in approximately 4-5 glasses of 12% wine. It is important to realize that a blood alcohol level does not represent the amount of alcohol consumed during an evening or a day, but is simply equivalent to the amount of alcohol in the system at the time a blood alcohol sample is taken. Furthermore, these amounts are only rough estimations.

Most ethyl alcohol is metabolized in the liver by the enzyme alcohol dehydrogenase. A small amount is also degraded by a second system, and approximately 10% is excreted by the lungs and in the urine. The rate of metabolism generally proceeds at zero-order kinetics which means the rate of elimination is constant no matter how much alcohol is in the system. At very high or very low concentrations, however, the rate may not follow standard zero-order kinetics. In general, approximately one ounce of alcohol is metabolized every hour or approximately 0.02 grams % per hour after peak concentration is achieved.

Numerous charts and graphs are available in standard texts which attempt to show how a person will be affected given a certain concentration of blood alcohol. These can be helpful in understanding general concepts of different levels of intoxication, but their use in reference to specific cases may be inaccurate. For example, most charts cite 0.5 grams % as a lethal concentration of alcohol. It is well known, however, that acutely intoxicated individuals may survive with much greater concentrations of alcohol.

Pathologists are often asked to interpret blood alcohol concentrations in the living as well as the dead. A medical examiner must be careful when attempting to estimate blood concentrations prior to the time a specimen was obtained. This is referred to as retrograde extrapolation and is often more difficult than it appears. There are many variables which make extrapolation more complex than using the rate of metabolism in reverse. For example, all liquors and wines are not absorbed at the same rate, and absorption rates may vary with individuals and amount of food within the stomach. One must estimate when the peak concentration occurred by considering how much an individual drank as well as the type of liquor and varieties and quantities of food consumed while drinking.

The pathology of alcoholism is impressive. Alcohol affects

most organ systems and chronic use can specifically produce one or more of the following pathological conditions: cirrhosis of the liver, pancreatitis, varices of the gastrointestinal tract, cardiac myopathy, and Wenicke's and Korsakoff's syndromes. Cancer is also the second leading cause of death in alcoholics (after cardiovascular disease) and the rate of carcinoma within this group is 10 times higher than expected of the general population.[2]

Alcoholics can die in many different ways. Chronic alcoholics may die suddenly without alcohol in their system and the only finding at autopsy may be a fatty liver. A death from any disease caused by chronic drinking is considered natural. In addition, chronic alcoholics are prone to hypothermia. If hypothermia is the cause of death, however, and alcoholism is a contributing factor, then the manner of death is accidental. Another example of an accidental death by alcohol is rapid consumption of a large amount causing respiratory depression.

Drugs of Abuse

There are many drugs of abuse. The most common ones seen during death investigation include: cocaine, heroin, morphine, codeine, Dilaudid, barbiturates, tricyclic antidepressants, marijuana, benzodiazepines, methadone, and phencyclidine. These drugs and chemicals may be the cause of death or an incidental finding.

The investigation of death by suspected drug abuse is slightly different than for other types of death because a pathologist must rely on toxicology results in order to determine the cause. An autopsy usually does not reveal a specific cause of death unless signs of previous abuse are present such as needle track marks and circular scars from skin popping. An autopsy may reveal a bolus of pills within the gastrointestinal tract in a suicide victim who did not live long after ingestion, or plastic packages (often condoms) filled with drugs as seen in "body packers" or "mules" who transport drugs. There may be considerable vascular congestion in the head and frothy white or blood-tinged material in the nose and airways. Internally, pulmonary edema is usually present in a drug overdose death. Other findings, such as heart disease, may also be present which may contribute to death.

The most important analysis needed from a postmortem exam is the result of a drug screen. Blood, bile, urine, and gastric contents should be submitted for analysis. Additional tissues, such as liver, kidney, heart, or fat may be necessary, especially if a more unusual drug is suspected. Vitreous humor may also be screened for drugs of abuse. The concentration of ethanol in the vitreous is approximately 10% higher than in blood due to a greater water content in the former. Toxicology lab personnel should understand their role in death investigation and the importance of working with a pathologist. A toxicologist's report will give a pathologist the types and amounts of drugs within various fluids and tissues analyzed. A report might also give an interpretation of whether an amount is in a toxic or therapeutic range, but it should not attempt to give a cause of death. There may be toxic concentrations of drugs in the system of a person who died from a completely unrelated cause.

Stimulants

Cocaine is a potent, naturally occurring, stimulant and one of the most commonly abused in this country. It alone accounts for hundreds of deaths investigated each year by large medical examiner jurisdictions. It can be sniffed, smoked (especially the crystallized form called "crack"), or taken intravenously. Cocaine is quickly metabolized in the blood stream to the metabolite benzoylecgonine which may be the only evidence suggesting a cause of death.

Within the past few years many studies have linked acute and chronic cocaine usage with different types of cardiovascular diseases. A cocaine abuser's heart may be larger than normal and have muscle scarring as well as signs of infarction. Sudden death associated with cocaine use may be due to a cardiac arrhythmia, myocardial infarction, or ruptured aneurysm. Occasionally, only small amounts of the drug are present, while at other times the amount is readily viewed as toxic. Furthermore, the drug may be so quickly metabolized that only benzoylecgonine is present. These situations should not dissuade a pathologist from thinking cocaine is the cause of death.

A recently described phenomenon called cocaine frenzy or cocaine psychosis can cause diagnostic difficulties. A cocaine abuser may unexpectedly become irrational, psychotic, physically violent, and abusive. The police are usually called to subdue the individual and, during the struggle, the person is at risk to die suddenly. A drug screen may reveal little cocaine in the system. When death occurs in this situation, relatives and friends are likely to make accusations of police brutality. If the medical examiner is unfamiliar with this entity, confusion and an inappropriate diagnosis may result.

Amphetamines are also stimulants commonly abused. They may be taken orally or intravenously. Recently, a new crystalline form called "ice" has been manufactured on the west coast. This very addictive form of amphetamine is still quite expensive and there has been limited use in all states.

Hypnotics, Depressants, and Analgesics

In large metropolitan areas, heroin, morphine, and analgesics such as Talwin, Dilaudid, and codeine were more popular before the use of cocaine became so widespread. In some jurisdictions, however, heroin abuse is increasing. In addition to being used alone, it is also used in combination with cocaine to maintain a "high" and soften a "crash." The mechanism of death from these classes of drugs is usually respiratory depression. Except in suicidal overdoses, in which there may be retention of pills in the stomach, there are no specific signs of an overdose at autopsy. As indicated above, there may be froth in the airways and pulmonary edema. These drugs can be found in combination with other dugs in both accidental and suicidal deaths. Deaths from intravenous injection tend not to be caused by a mixture of drugs.

Hallucinogens

LSD is rarely a sole cause of death. It may be important, however, in circumstances surrounding a death such as the cause of irrational and careless behavior. On the other hand, PCP is a commonly encountered street drug which alone can cause death. It is both a stimulant and a depressant which has been associated with bizarre outbursts similar to the frenzy described with cocaine.

References:

1. For example, Baselt's Disposition of Toxic Drugs and Chemicals in Man.
2. Schuckit MA: Alcohol and Alcoholism. In Isselbacher KJ, et al (eds): Harrison's Principles of Internal Medicine, 13th ed. New York, McGraw-Hill, Inc., p. 2422.

Asphyxia And Drowning
Asphyxia

Asphyxia means death due to lack of oxygen to the brain. The following are the different ways a person can asphyxiate:
1. Compression of the neck
2. Blockage of the airway (suffocation, gagging)
3. Compression of the chest or airway (postural asphyxia)
4. Chemical (lack of available oxygen)

Compression of the neck

Probably the best-known type of asphyxia is neck compression by hanging, a common means of suicide. An individual will loop or tie rope, wire, or articles of clothing around his neck and hang himself. Pressure on the neck will usually occlude the vasculature, but not necessarily the airway (larynx or trachea). A person will become unconscious and die if blood is prevented from going to the brain or returning to the heart. Very little pressure is needed to occlude the veins returning blood from the brain to the heart. It is a misconception that the airway must be occluded to asphyxiate. Ruptured blood vessels in lower extremities, called Tardieu spots, are common.

The neck can also be compressed manually by strangulation or throttling. An assailant must compress the airway or blood vessels to render a victim unconscious. The time it takes to render someone unconscious depends on the location of pressure. For example, if pressure is applied over the carotid sinus, located just below the angle of the jaw, a victim may become unconscious in a matter of seconds due to bradycardia. This would be an unusual mechanism of death in manual strangulation. The time from application of pressure to the neck and unconsciousness will be longer if pressure is exerted over the anterior neck. In this instance, the trachea would be compressed or the base of the tongue would be forced backwards and upwards to occlude the airway. In general, the time it takes to render an individual unconscious is quite variable. Furthermore, after a victim is unconscious, pressure must be continued before death ensues. This time is also variable, but again can be measured in minutes before irreversible brain damage occurs. In such cases, one should not give an opinion as to the exact time it took someone to die. Although there may be minimal bodily injuries in manual strangulation, signs of trauma to the neck are generally evident. There may be contusions or abrasions but rarely lacerations. Superficial cuts from fingernails, either the victim's or the assailant's, may be present. Careful internal examination of the neck is required to locate areas of soft tissue hemorrhage. The tongue, hyoid bone, and larynx should be removed and carefully examined. Hemorrhage in the tongue caused by biting, and fractures of the hyoid, are often found in cases of manual strangulation. The neck is best examined in a layerwise dissection after the internal organs and brain have been removed.

External injuries to the neck in suicidal hanging may be much more obvious than internal ones. The object used to compress the neck often leaves an abraded, imprinted mark. If a ligature is thin like a rope, a depressed mark on the neck is usually apparent and the pattern can be matched to a particular ligature. If the ligature is wide like a towel or shirt, however, the mark may have a nonspecific pattern. Many hangings do not cause internal hemorrhages in the soft tissues of the neck. A person could still die of asphyxiation but the circumstances surrounding death need to be analyzed to correctly interpret the injuries.

Pinpoint hemorrhages, or petechiae, are commonly present in the eyes after manual compression of the neck. They arise when the increased vascular pressure causes capillaries to rupture. Petechiae may be found on either the bulbar or palpebrae conjunctivae, and face, especially the forehead and around the eyes. They are not often found in suicidal hanging. It is important to note that petechiae are not specific for asphyxiation and may occur in people who die suddenly from other causes such as heart disease.

Autoerotic deaths

A unique subgroup of strangulation deaths are autoerotic deaths which occur during purposeful attempts to reduce blood flow to the brain by neck compression with the intent of heightening sexual pleasure. Any object which compresses the neck can be used. Most of the time a towel or some soft object is placed between the ligature and the neck to prevent visible scrapes or bruises. The diagnosis is readily made at the scene because the decedent is usually naked with pornographic material nearby. Often there is evidence of repeated behavior at the scene, such as worn grooves in the rafters where ropes or pulleys have been placed. This situation is ruled an accident, not a suicide.

Blockage of the airway (suffocation, aspiration, gagging)

If the airway is blocked then oxygen cannot get into the lungs and asphyxiation results. A pillow or hand, for instance, can be placed over the mouth, prevent a person from breathing, and cause suffocation. An unchewed peanut or small parts of toys can become lodged in an infant's or child's trachea. Individuals without teeth or with a history of stroke or other debilitating disease may have trouble chewing and aspirate food into their airway. Those under the influence of alcohol are also more likely to aspirate. There are usually no signs of trauma in these deaths. The diagnosis requires a complete autopsy which includes a complete examination of the neck, mouth, and oropharynx.

Compression of the chest or airway (postural asphyxia)

Postural asphyxiation occurs when a person cannot breathe because of an inability to move one's chest. This type of circumstance is commonly seen during motor vehicle accidents. For example a car may overturn on a victim or a driver may become trapped between the steering wheel and seat. There may be surprisingly few injuries except for other signs of blunt trauma which do not relate to the cause of death. Other common scenarios include: a mechanic compressed beneath a car which has fallen from its supports, an infant wedged between a crib railing and an ill-fitting mattress, and an intoxicated individual who collapses to "sleep it off" in a position that compromises his airway. Petechiae, dusky coloration of the face and chest, and pulmonary edema are often present. The circumstances surrounding a death are critical when attempting to determine the cause and manner of death in these cases.

Chemical (lack of available oxygen)

If the atmosphere's oxygen is replaced by another chemical or gas, or if a person's red blood cells are unable to deliver oxygen to bodily tissues, a person will asphyxiate. Depletion of atmospheric oxygen usually occurs in a relatively closed environment. Gas accumulation, for instance, can displace oxygen in improperly vented mine shafts, sewers, or chemical storage tanks. It is common to encounter multiple deaths in such cases because rescuers can also be overcome by fumes and lack of oxygen.

Carbon monoxide (CO) and cyanide are examples of chemical asphyxia by interfering with oxygen delivery to the tissues. When a car is left running in a closed garage, CO from burning gasoline competes with oxygen for binding to hemoglobin on the red blood cells. CO is an odorless, tasteless gas which forms when carbon is burned and has a binding capacity over 200 times that of oxygen. The result is asphyxiation because no oxygen is carried to the brain. CO can incapacitate a person very quickly. A 4-5% atmospheric concentration is fatal to an adult within minutes and to a child even more quickly. The concentration of CO found in the system of an individual dying from CO exposure may be as high as 70-80%. This concentration may be much lower, especially in a person with preexisting natural disease. Blood remains red, producing the characteristic cherry red color of livor mortis, because CO binds tightly to hemoglobin. CO poisoning is a common means of suicide in many parts of this country. It is also the cause of death in fire victims. Fire deaths will be discussed further in the next chapter.

Cyanide causes asphyxiation by interfering with cytochrome oxidase and other cellular enzyme systems which the body needs for the utilization of oxygen. Livor mortis will be red as in carbon monoxide poisoning. Pathologists frequently make the diagnosis by odor at autopsy because the gas smells like bitter almonds.

Drowning

The diagnosis of drowning is one of exclusion. There are no drowning tests to prove a person drowned and an autopsy is inconclusive. The body is usually wet or is found in water to make the diagnosis. There may be injuries from being in the water, such as tears and scrapes of the skin from impacts against boats or bridges. Occasionally, in salt water drownings, marine life may feed on the skin of the face, especially around the mouth, nose, and ears. Abrasions may be found on the forehead, knees, and backs of hands from a body scraping against the bottom of the lake or pool.

Healthy individuals rarely drown unless there is an intervening reason to make them less likely to survive in water such as drugs or natural disease. If heart disease is present, a person may or may not have drowned. For example, a man seen clutching his chest shortly before falling out of a boat may not have drowned. If a witness states that a man went in the water and did not struggle or come up then he probably died from a cardiac arrhythmia before he drowned. This type of case must be based on a witnessed account. In another example, a woman found submerged in a bathtub without signs of injury or struggle probably had a fatal arrhythmia rather than drowned because she would have been able to get out of the tub.

At autopsy a pathologist may find hemorrhage in the ear drums, water in the stomach, and fluid in the lungs. Laymen refer to this fluid as "water in the lungs," but drowning victims may or may not have heavy, wet lungs. If a person dies in fresh water, a hypotonic environment, inhaled water may be pumped by the heart throughout the circulation because of a lower

79

osmolarity of water. On the other hand, if a person drowns in salt water, a hypertonic environment, the lungs may become quite heavy because fluid from the circulation diffuses into the lungs caused by the water's high salt content and higher osmolarity. A decedent may also have "dry" lungs because in a small percentage of drownings the larynx may undergo spasm preventing water from entering the lungs.

Electrical and Thermal Injury and Exposure to Extreme Temperatures
Electrocution

Electrocution is not always an easy diagnosis to make. The history and circumstances of death are vitally important because low voltage deaths frequently cause no injuries on the body. On the other hand, high voltage deaths are easier to diagnose because of obvious burn injuries.

The cause of death from electrocution is related to the amount of current (or amperage) flowing through a body. The amperage is equal to the voltage (or charge) divided by the ohms (or resistance)(amperage=volts/ohms). Increasing the amperage by raising the voltage or lowering the resistance makes the contact more dangerous. Although both direct and alternating currents can be lethal, most deaths occur from contact with alternating currents having low voltages such as 110 or 220 usually found in homes.

There needs to be a complete circuit from the power source to the ground for death to occur. A person will not become electrocuted if he is insulated from the ground. The direction the path takes in the body determines whether shock will be fatal. An arrhythmia is likely if current travels through the heart, especially if amperage is low. For example, current may travel up an arm, across the heart, and exit through the other arm and hand. Respiratory arrest may occur when current travels through the respiratory center of the brain.

Contact with standard household current amperage depends mainly on the resistance of that part of the body touching a hot wire. A hand or foot with thickened calloused skin offers more resistance than skin on the rest of the body. Moisture will decrease resistance. Skin with resistance of over 900 ohms may be decreased to 200-300 ohms after it is wet.

External and internal injuries vary tremendously in electrocutions. The extent of external wound damage is dependent upon the amount of current and its duration. If a current is spread over a wide contact for a short duration there will not be any injuries to the skin. Clothing may be damaged so it must be retained for examination. Low voltage tends to cause easily overlooked small burns especially on the hands and the feet. The lesions may be red and inconspicuous, umbilicated, or depressed with firm white centers and brown and red serpiginous edges. High voltage deaths usually leave easily recognizable, deeply charred areas. Lesions may be present at the entrance and/or exit sites.

Internal injuries are rarely seen in low voltage deaths. These changes may be nonspecific and include pulmonary edema, petechiae in the eyes, and hemorrhages in the outflow track of the heart. Higher voltage trauma may cause heat effects and burning to the organs directly under the point of exit or entrance.

Since many people are electrocuted by low voltage, there may be no evidence of injury. The diagnosis is made by careful investigation of the circumstances surrounding the scene of death such as an individual who dies while taking a bath because an electrical appliance falls into the water. If no information from the scene is available, a pathologist would probably sign out the case as unknown.

If someone dies while working with electrical equipment, the equipment needs to be tested by a qualified individual. It is not difficult to determine if the equipment has a short circuit. The circuitry of a house needs to be checked if faulty wiring is suspected. These are necessary for arriving at a correct cause of death, identifying faulty machinery and products, and protecting other individuals in the environment.

Fire Deaths

Most fire deaths are due to carbon monoxide poisoning, not direct thermal injury. As discussed in the section on asphyxia, exposure to CO can be fatal within minutes. Thermal effects to the body may be slight or severe. The degree of heat does not dictate how long a person survives during a fire. The extent of damage depends on the length of time a decedent is exposed to flames and how close a body is to a fire.

The most important factor in any fire death investigation is determining whether an individual was dead before a fire started (suspected homicide) or if a decedent succumbed because of a fire. Measurement of CO is probably most helpful in this regard. If the hemoglobin saturation is greater than 10% CO then a person was alive and inhaled the atmosphere during the fire. People who smoke may have a CO of 10% or less. CO content of blood should always be measured regardless if the injuries are extreme, the organs appear bright red, or there is much soot in the airway. Occasionally the CO will be negative as is in an explosion which can cause death rapidly. A negative CO might initially be confusing but a quality scene investigation should resolve any problems. In addition, there will usually be soot in the mouth, nose and airways below the upper larynx if a person was alive and breathing during a fire.

Individuals may die later in the hospital from complications of burns, such as inhalation injury to the lungs and trachea, hypoxia, fluid and electrolyte disorders, and infections. Skin burns may range from partial or full thickness to charring and incineration. The extent and degree of injury should be described at autopsy.

In very hot fires, much of the head and distal extremities may be incinerated. Abdominal and thoracic organs may be exposed. Intense heat may produce thermal fractures and exposed bones will be brittle. Although thermal fractures can be recognized, care must be maintained by a pathologist in determining if fractures are postmortem. The presence of coagulated blood in the epidural space is a heat-induced artifact.

All fire deaths should be x-rayed so that foreign objects will not be overlooked. Blood can usually be obtained from a body no matter how badly it is burned. If no blood is available, a pathologist may have to submit sections of the spleen or skeletal muscle.

Hyperthermia

Very few signs at autopsy will indicate a person died from hyperthermia. The most important sign is body temperature. If a body is found at a scene soon after death, an increased temperature will be evident. If a decedent is not found for many hours, or is discovered the next day, a diagnosis may be impossible. In summer, however, a body may be transported to the morgue in a warm vehicle. If that vehicle does not go directly to the morgue and the body heats up, a diagnosis will not be possible from body examination alone. Therefore, scene investigation is a necessity.

There are a number of causes of hyperthermia. Older people may succumb to heat during summer months because of an underlying disease which contributes to their inability to cope with heat, or their dwellings may not have an appropriate cooling system.

Malignant hyperthermia is a syndrome which develops in people who react to certain drugs, such a phenothiozines or halothane. The use of cocaine is also associate with hyperthermia. In some of these cases there is a genetic predisposition toward developing the syndrome.

Hypothermia

Like hyperthermia, the elderly and those individuals with underlying disease are more likely to suffer from hypothermia. People can die from improperly heated homes or apartments or if they are caught outside in the cold. Alcoholics can become hypothermic if they fall asleep in the cold while inebriated. Nursing home patients can succumb to the cold after becoming confused and walking outdoors during winter months.

Autopsy findings are few. There are usually no findings unless an individual has a natural disease or is under the influence of drugs or alcohol. Necrotizing pancreatitis occurs rarely in cases of death due to hypothermia. Superficial hemorrhages of the gastric mucosa are more commonly present.

An entity called "paradoxical undressing" is occasionally encountered. A person may begin to undress while dying from the cold. This may appear suspicious if the decedent is a naked woman found outside with her clothes scattered about. An initial impression may suggest sexual assault. Further investigation should uncover the correct manner and cause of death.

Blunt Trauma
General And Motor Vehicle–Pedestrian
General

The characteristic injuries of blunt trauma are contusions, abrasions, and lacerations. Abrasions occur externally whereas contusions and lacerations may be external or internal.

Contusions (Bruises)

Contusions are discolorations of the skin caused by bleeding into the tissues from ruptured blood vessels. The application of sufficient pressure to the skin surface causes disruption of blood vessels without breaking the skin. In general, the older a person, the easier the vessels will rupture. There is no way, however, to determine exactly how much force is needed to produce a contusion. The age of a contusion is difficult to determine because of the great variability of a body's reaction to trauma. For example, an older individual may bruise more easily and resolution of bruises generally takes longer. People with blood disorders and liver disease may develop more severe contusions than healthy individuals. Depending on the size of the bruise, it may completely reabsorb in several weeks or linger for several months. A contusion changes color as hemoglobin undergoes degradation. The color progresses from blue or red, to red-blue, to green, to brown, and finally yellow. These color changes, however, may appear out of order and may overlap. There is no way to know how long each color stage lasts. Occasionally a recent contusion has a brown tinge. The color of the edge of a bruise usually is the best indicator of age, the oldest color being at the edge.

In addition to the gross appearances, pathologists have attempted to age bruises by examining microscopic sections. Once again, the edge, which is the oldest or most organized part of a bruise, is the best part to examine. Changes which aid in age determination include: the degree and type of inflammation, pigment deposition, and the degree of scarring. Most of the time the question is whether an injury is acute or chronic. That is, did the contusion happen at the time of death or at some other significant reference time? Unfortunately, aging contusions is not exact and can often be misleading. For example, a bruise on the scalp may look as if it occurred at about the time of death by both gross and microscopic examination but actually may be days old. As in other situations, a pathologist considers the scene investigation and historical information and will not make conclusions based solely on autopsy findings.

Abrasions

An abrasion is denuded skin caused by friction. A wound may be either deep or superficial depending on the force and the coarseness of the surface which caused the abrasion. Occasionally, the direction of the force can be determined. If one end of a wound has margins with raised skin, for example, the force originated from the opposite side. The characteristics of an abrasion can help define the type of surface that caused the wound. For instance, a person who slid across pavement might have a deeper and rougher wound than a person who slid across a rug.

Lacerations (Tears)

Tears of the skin due to pressure are called lacerations. By definition, a wound called a laceration means that it was produced by blunt trauma. It does not, however, imply how the trauma occurred. Many tears are associated with both contusions and abrasions. For example, a blow to the head with a hammer may cause tearing of the scalp and an adjacent abrasion. If blood escapes into the surrounding tissues, the skin can also appear bruised.

A laceration must be distinguished from an incision. A laceration usually has bridges of tissue connecting one side of the wound to the other. Cutting and incised wounds have no tissue bridges because a sharp object cuts the wound cleanly from the top to the bottom of the wound.

Deaths due to blunt trauma may have some or none of the above external signs of trauma, particularly with blows to the abdomen. In some cases there are no external signs of a traumatic death. The situation and circumstances surrounding a death will usually yield clues that an autopsy is necessary.

Motor Vehicle and Pedestrian Injuries

Blunt force injuries sustained by occupants of motor vehicles can be complex. In general, an effort should be made to correlate injury patterns with objects found in or on a car. When a motor vehicle is involved in an accident, the driver and passengers move towards the site of the impact. For example, an impact to the front left of a car during a head-on crash causes occupants to move to the left, especially if unrestrained. The driver may hit the steering wheel, dashboard or windshield, and the passengers the dashboard, windshield or rearview mirror. Each will have significant injuries even though they hit different objects.

Certain injuries are particularly common and characteristic. For example, blunt impact to the chest from a steering wheel may leave very few external marks, but result in a tear of the aorta when the body decelerates rapidly as it strikes the dashboard or steering wheel. The heart and upper aorta, being relatively mobile, continue to travel toward the front of the chest while the rest of the body rapidly decelerates. This causes a shearing effect which tears the aorta at its point of attachment, just distal to the left subclavian artery. In some cases the heart can be avulsed from its attachments.

Windshield and side window glass cause characteristic injuries. A windshield is composed of two pieces of glass bonded together with plastic. This glass shatters on impact but remains together in pieces by the plastic layer. Thus, an occupant's head rarely goes through a windshield. Side windows are made of tempered glass which shatters during impact into numerous small fragments. These fragments cause a characteristic "dicing" pattern of lacerated-abrasions on the face, shoulders, or arms. Observation of this pattern is one method of determining an occupant's position. A driver has dicing injuries on the left side of his body and a passenger has them on the right.

Other common injuries involve fractures of the patella and femur caused by hitting a dashboard. Needless to say, high speed collisions can cause multiple severe injuries. There may be extensive skull fractures, cerebral contusions, subscapular hemorrhages, facial lacerations, contusions, and abrasions. Common injuries to the trunk include: rib and pelvic fractures, and lacerations of the lungs, liver, and spleen due to impact and sudden deceleration. Lacerations of these internal organs may occur without associated rib fractures. Strap-like abrasions may be produced by seat belts. If any of the occupants are ejected during a crash, obviously the injuries may be quite variable and very severe. Head trauma is common in these situations. In addition, when an occupant is ejected, a vehicle may roll over him and cause compressive asphyxia, often with few other injuries.

Pedestrian fatalities also have characteristic injury patterns. It is important to study these patterns and compare them to how an accident allegedly occurred. In a hit-and-run fatality, a study of the injuries may help identify the vehicle. The points of impact on a body are particularly important and clothing must be closely examined for paint chips and parts of the vehicle that may be transferred on impact. Bumper impact sites on the legs should be measured from the heel. This will indicate the direction from which the deceased was hit, and the height will correlate with the height of the bumper. A bumper fracture is often triangular in shape with the apex of the triangle pointing in the direction that a vehicle was moving. When the brakes are applied, a bumper fracture occurs low because the front end of the car drops. When hit by a car, an adult pedestrian will be lifted up and may strike the windshield or roof or be thrown over the car. Children who have a lower center of gravity than adults tend to be propelled to the ground and are often run over resulting in many points of impact and various injuries. Often clothing and tissues can adhere to the undercarriage of a vehicle. All these injuries must be analyzed and matched to damaged parts of the vehicle. Occasionally, points of impact will leave a pattern which may indicate a particular make of a vehicle.

Blunt Head Trauma

The examination and description of head trauma should proceed from the scalp to the skull and brain. This orientation aids a pathologist in making sure all injuries are properly recorded. It also enables a reader of the autopsy report to have a much clearer understanding of the trauma.

External Injuries

Blunt trauma to the scalp and face can produce contusions, lacerations, and abrasions that differ from those occurring on the rest of the body because of irregular surfaces of the head. For example, due to underlying bone, pressure from blunt trauma may cause the skin to tear and appear as if a person was cut or stabbed.

There may be no external signs of trauma to the head if a person has a full head of hair which acts to shield the skin surface from markings. Obvious external injuries are not necessary for a death to be caused by head trauma. This is one important reason autopsies need to be performed when the cause of death is in doubt.

In addition, there are two common signs of head trauma. The first, known as Battle's sign, is a bluish discoloration of the skin behind the ear that occurs from blood leaking under the scalp after a fracture involving the petrous portions of the temporal bone. The second is called a spectacle hemorrhage or raccoon's eyes. This is a discoloration of the tissues around the eyes due to a basilar skull fracture of the anterior fossa. The hemorrhages may involve one or both eyes and may be mistakenly interpreted as if the decedent had been struck about the face and eyes.

Scalp Injuries and Skull Fractures

As mentioned above, the external surface of the scalp may not show evidence of blunt trauma. If a blow is severe enough to cause death, however, hemorrhage occurs on the underside of the scalp (subscapular hemorrhages). The number of hemorrhages gives an examiner the fewest number of times an individual sustained an impact. When there are multiple blows to the same general area an exact number may not be discernable because the hemorrhages coalesce.

Skull fractures may be comminuted, depressed, or linear.

There may be one or more fractures which can be simple or extend completely through the bone. Occasionally, a depressed fracture leaves a patterned injury allowing determination of the weapon used or surface a victim contacted. A heavy object with a small surface area like a hammer is much more likely to leave a definitive pattern than one of the same weight with a larger surface area. Most fractures are usually from a direct impact injury. A person can also have a skull fracture opposite a point of impact, a so-called contrecoup fracture. Contrecoup means opposite the blow. For example, if a person falls and hits the back of his head, he may have a contrecoup fracture on the interior portion of the skull near his forehead. It is important to note that a fracture need not be present for head trauma to be fatal.

Hemorrhages over the Surface of the Brain

Bleeding can be present in three locations over the surface and coverings of the brain: epidural, subdural, and subarachnoid. Subdural and subarachnoid hemorrhages may occur from traumatic and natural disease. An epidural hemorrhage, however, is traumatic until proven otherwise.

Epidural Hemorrhage

Blood directly beneath the skull and on top of the dura is an epidural hemorrhage. Epidural hemorrhages result from skull fractures which lacerate blood vessels in underlying vascular channels. The most frequently involved vessel is the middle meningeal artery which traverses the thin temporal bone.

After a vessel ruptures, blood accumulates in the epidural space. Since the skull is a closed space, the cranial vault cannot accept much extra volume before pressure on the brain causes death. An extra 100 milliliters of blood in the cranial vault usually causes major problems, especially if it accumulates quickly. A disc-shaped hematoma causes pressure on the dura which in turn compresses the brain. An epidural hematoma usually accumulates quickly since the bleeding is arterial. An individual with an epidural hemorrhage may become symptomatic within minutes or hours depending on the rate of bleeding.

Subdural Hemorrhage

In contrast to the epidural hemorrhage, a subdural bleed occurs from veins, not arteries. Thus, the bleeding tends to be slower than the arterial bleed although acute subdural hemorrhages may bring about symptoms just as quickly as epidural bleeds. These hemorrhages occur because of ruptured bridging veins which traverse the subdural space from the brain to the dura. Blood accumulates in a uniform fashion over the brain surface but is not limited by the dura and does not focally compress the brain. Subdural hemorrhages are usually caused by trauma. Acute hemorrhages are usually related to trauma but any subarachnoid hemorrhage can rupture through the arachnoid layer and extend into the subdural space. Examples would be a ruptured arteriovenous malformation or berry aneurysm. If caused by trauma, subdural hemorrhages may be unilateral or bilateral and do not necessarily have to be on the same side as the impact.

Since the bleeding can be slow, a subdural hemorrhage may become a chronic condition. If a person has had a subdural bleeding episode months or years prior to death, the area where the bleeding occurred will be encircled by a thick fibrous membrane which essentially walls off the hematoma. The subsequent pressure on the brain will flatten it over a large area. The age of a chronic subdural hemorrhage which heals on its own can be determined with the aid of a microscope. Within a few days, specialized cells called fibroblasts begin to grow around the area of bleeding. Depending on the size of the hematoma, the organization process may take weeks to months before there is a rigid membrane completely encircling the hematoma. Eventually all of the blood is reabsorbed and the subdural hemorrhage appears as a thin brown-yellow membrane. These sites are prone to rebleed.

Subarachnoid Hemorrhage

This is the most common type of hemorrhage from trauma and is often associated with more serious trauma such as skull fractures. Relatively little force, however, is required to cause rupture of capillaries over the surface of the brain in the subarachnoid space. This type of hemorrhage is also seen during a violent hyperextension of the head which can tear vessels at the base of the brain. Similar traumatic subarachnoid hemorrhages result from a blow to the side of the head which tears the vertebral artery. This rapid release of blood into the subarachnoid space can cause sudden collapse and death. Subarachnoid hemorrhage can also result from the rupture of a berry aneurysm of the vessels at the base of the brain. This is usually considered a natural event but may occasionally be precipitated by trauma.

Concussion

A concussion is the result of blunt trauma to the head which causes disorientation, unconsciousness, or death. When an individual receives a concussion there are no visible signs of damage to the brain by gross or microscopic examination. Fatal concussions are most likely due to sudden disruptions of vital nerve connections in the brainstem, a structure connecting the main part of the brain to the spinal cord. In these cases, an investigation and knowledge of circumstances surrounding a death is critical because an autopsy will usually be negative or reveal only a few signs of external blunt trauma.

Contusions

Contusions are small hemorrhages produced by a rupture of capillaries. Contusions can be classified depending on their location and relationships to other injuries. Some are dependent on the movement of the head at the time of impact, while others are not. The contusions most important to a pathologist and which are dependent on the status of the head at impact are: coup, contrecoup, and intermediate. (see Figures 1 and 2)

Coup - The head is stationary and the object which strikes the head is moving. The contusion is directly beneath the point of impact on the scalp.

Contrecoup -The head is moving (i.e. falling) and the object is stationary. The contusion is located directly opposite the point of impact.

Intermediate - The head is moving and the top strikes a stationary object. The contusions are distributed throughout the brain and brainstem.

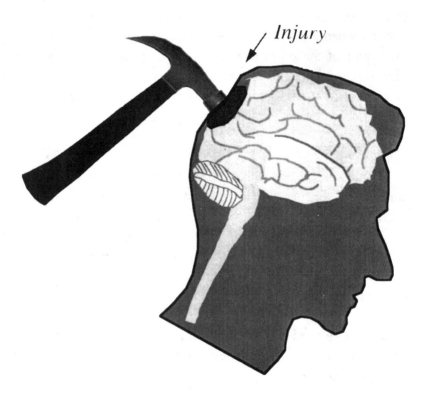

Figure 1. Coup contusion

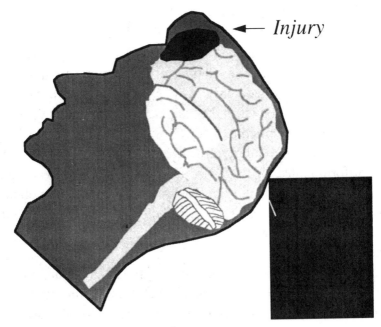

Figure 2. Contrecoup contusion

Spinal Cord Injuries

Injuries to the spinal cord may be similar to those in the brain. Severe injuries causing hemorrhage around the cord may be easily seen but contusions may be difficult to recognize grossly. They may be faint and visible only with the aid of a microscope. They are usually eccentrically located and rarely midline. Midline defects are more often secondary complications and usually occur in a person who survived for a period of time. Most injuries of the cord are due to subluxations and not fractures of the vertebral column. Subluxations and fractures cause pressure on the spinal cord with subsequent

97

injury such as bleeding and contusions.

Complications of Trauma

The three major complications of head trauma are infection, hemorrhage, and edema. Any open wound can become infected. Open wounds in the brain rarely occur unless there is a skull fracture. Occasionally fractures may be small and difficult to diagnose, particularly fractures of the middle fossa and cribriform plates. A diagnosed infection of the brain is usually accompanied by a history of trauma several days before clinical symptoms become apparent. A pathologist must ensure that the dura is stripped away from the bone in order to identify the defect.

Unexpected hemorrhages into injuries can occur in many circumstances. For example, a subdural hemorrhage can rebleed. Any person who has hypertension, liver disease, or a blood disorder may bleed into a previously injured area like a contusion.

Brain swelling is commonly associated with head trauma. The swelling may be mild or cause considerable distortion of the brain, both grossly and microscopically. Brain weight is occasionally used by some pathologists to assess brain swelling but is rarely reliable.

Pediatric Forensic Pathology

Investigating fatalities in children requires special expertise because injury patterns are different than in adults and may be quite subtle. Children who are repeatedly battered may present with multiple types and ages of injuries. Some may have no visible external injuries but have fatal organ damage internally, such as a ruptured liver. There may be few or no injuries to the head as in the case of a baby who is violently shaken. The history is essential to a correct diagnosis in all battered children cases and sudden infant deaths. The medical personnel who first see these children and interact with their families have the best opportunity to find out from the caregiver what occurred. A family member will often tell physicians and nurses a different story than is later told to the police or death investigator. All statements should be recorded shortly after they have been made. Frequently, the history of how an injury occurred is inconsistent with the pattern and type of injury discovered by a medical examiner.

Battered Child Syndrome

These children have a history of being repeatedly beaten by a caregiver. The injuries occur over a period of weeks, months, and years. Usually there are numerous injuries of different ages. It is common to see a child with healing rib fractures and old contusions in addition to the recent injuries which caused death. The external injuries to the head from blunt trauma may only be visible on the undersurface of the scalp. Contusions of the trunk may be readily apparent or absent even though there are fatal injuries to the internal organs. A pathologist describes all injuries, not just the ones which are thought to be fatal, since the timing and number of injuries are of legal importance.

Fracture sites should be examined grossly and may be examined microscopically. Since a fracture may be missed during a postmortem examination it is useful to take x-rays. A whole body series should be performed and, if an examiner is not expert in reviewing radiographs, a radiologist should be consulted. All injuries should be photographed.

Injuries to the trunk causing death generally take the form of lacerations and hemorrhages to the visceral organs such as liver, spleen, and pancreas in addition to the colon, small intestine, and mesentery. All of these injuries and the development of the complications such as infection may occur without any signs of external trauma. A blow to the abdomen, for instance, may not cause an injury to the skin. Abdominal skin is elastic and compressible and does not cover a firm organ or bone against which the skin can be compressed to rupture blood vessels and produce a contusion.

Since blunt trauma may be widely distributed over a body, all suspicious areas of skin need to be reflected, including the back, thighs, and buttocks to make certain that areas of old or recent hemorrhage are not overlooked.

Cases of intentional asphyxiation may be encountered, although they are not common. Caregivers have been known to force a child to inhale food and seasonings which may become lodged in airways. A single piece of food stuck in the airway may not appear suspicious, but a handful of pepper within the nose and mouth would be difficult to explain as an accident.

Signs of sexual abuse should be noted, even if these injuries had nothing to do with the cause of death. Bite marks or other injuries may involve the vagina, hymen, or penis. The diagnosis of anal dilatation as a sign of sexual abuse should be made cautiously because anal sphincters become lax after death. Venereal warts and presence of sperm are obvious indications of sexual abuse.

Shaken Baby

Shaking a child or an infant may cause a fatal head injury without external marks. An infant's head is poorly stabilized by weak neck muscles. Violent anterior and posterior motions may cause nerve damage, brain swelling, minor bleeding, and retinal hemorrhages. Moreover, an examiner may discover contusions on the arms or chest where an infant was grabbed while being shaken.

A child may become unconscious within minutes of the violent act and will die if not treated quickly. Since there may be no obvious signs of abuse, emergency room personnel may not be suspicious of any foul play. An investigation should be conducted, however, on any child who is dead on arrival to an emergency room.

Neglect

Children do not need to be battered with multiple internal and external injuries for a medical examiner to rule a death a homicide. Child abuse and death can result from neglect. For example, if a child is not fed or if a child is left in a harmful, unsupervised situation, death may occur.

If a child is malnourished, his skin may be lax with little underlying soft tissue, he may appear underweight for his age, and his eyes may appear sunken. Internally, there will be scant fatty tissue and no food or feces in the gastrointestinal tract. Vitreous humor should be collected and analyzed for electrolytes (such as chloride, sodium, and potassium) whenever dehydration is suspected because it can confirm the suspicions of the gross examination. For the diagnosis of dehydration, vitreous sodium and chloride should be greater than 155 mEq and 13 mEq, respectively.

A caregiver may also be found guilty of homicide if a child is left in a dangerous situation. For example, if a baby is left unattended in a car with the windows closed for hours during the summer months, a child may quickly become overheated and expire. This could be viewed as a death from neglect and may be ruled an accident or homicide by a medical examiner.

Sudden Infant Death Syndrome (Crib Death)

Approximately seven children per 100,000 births or 6,000 – 7,000 children die unexpectedly each year with an unrevealing autopsy and scene investigation. If death occurs within the first year or so of life the death is diagnosed as Sudden Infant Death Syndrome (SIDS). There may be a history of an upper respiratory infection within the previous week of a child's death, without serious illness or symptoms. Statistical analyses have noted an association of prematurity, smoking mothers, and lower socioeconomic living circumstances with this type of death, but none of these are present in every case. Despite many years of scientific research in this area, SIDS cannot be predicted or prevented.

A diagnosis of SIDS requires a complete autopsy and scene investigation. An autopsy without an adequate scene investigation presents a medical examiner with a problem because a negative autopsy does not confirm that a child died of SIDS. A child who is accidentally suffocated by becoming wedged between a mattress and bars of a crib, or an infant who is intentionally suffocated, may have a negative autopsy. Without a good scene investigation and history the best diagnosis cannot be made. Unfortunately, in some areas of the country there is no scene investigation and sometimes no postmortem examination. Clearly, a diagnosis of SIDS in these situations is unwarranted.

In SIDS, an autopsy may reveal nonspecific and nondiagnostic changes such as petechiae of the heart, lung, and thymus. The lungs may be edematous and congested and there may be insignificant microscopic foci of inflammation. Occasionally pathologists differ about how much disease must be present before another diagnosis besides SIDS can be made. These differences are not as important as assuring whether or not there was foul play.

A diagnosis of SIDS is quite significant to a family who is trying to cope with the grief and guilt associated with an unexpected loss of a child. A medical examiner has the opportunity to be of help to these families by explaining that the death was not due to inadequate care and by referring them to appropriate SIDS counselors.

PART III
Forensic DNA Testing

Introduction

Forensic DNA testing has been used in criminal and non-criminal cases since 1985.[1] Its evolution parallels the diagnostic capabilities that emerged from the field of molecular biology. At its inception, DNA testing could only be performed by laboratories with molecular diagnostic capabilities. The credibility and reliability of these laboratories needed to be established, as did standardized procedures for handling samples. As is often the case with new technology, skepticism was high as critics cautioned against the science and technology as well as the statistics and population genetics.

Presently, molecular diagnostic techniques are more commonly used. The polymerase chain reaction (PCR), for instance, can be performed by numerous research and clinical labs, and standards and quality control protocols have become firmly established. Moreover, the Committee on DNA Technology in Forensic Science has published their recommendations.[2] Since that report, the technical reliability of DNA evidence has been unanimously accepted by the U.S. courts.[3] Even the applied statistics to establish frequencies or likelihood of a match between a suspect and criminal evidence, for instance, are conservative estimates as outlined by the Committee.[2] Consequently, the likelihood of criticizing the applied statistics of forensic DNA testing, the "weakest" aspect to some because statistics is often viewed as a "soft science," has been virtually eliminated.

Most of all, the public needs to understand that the forensic DNA testing controversy has been resolved. There is no scientific reason to doubt the accuracy of forensic DNA typing results, provided that the testing laboratory and the specific tests are on a par with currently practiced standards in the field.[3]

This chapter is not intended to be an encyclopedic overview of forensic DNA testing. The subject matter, however, is technical and the jargon can be confusing, especially when abbreviated (e.g., PCR, RFLP, VNTR). For those who want more information about a technical issue, the author suggests choosing a source written by scientists trained in molecular biology. There are several outstanding texts in this field that are user-friendly such as Molecular Biology of the Cell, Genes V, and Recombinant DNA. Many excellent review articles have appeared in *Scientific American*, *The New England Journal of Medicine,* and *Clinics in Laboratory Medicine* that are clear and concise. In this field, where terminology can be an enemy, it is critical that accurate definitions of molecular biology terms are used. This is especially true for attorneys who need to use DNA evidence in court. A sound foundation will build a stronger and far more effective case.

DNA Structure

Nucleic acids are the genetic material of all organisms. The two types of nucleic acids are deoxyribonucleic acid (DNA) and ribonucleic acid (RNA). DNA is the genetic material for most organisms including humans; RNA is involved in protein synthesis and is also the genetic material for some viruses. DNA is packaged into a mass of chromatin in the nucleus when the cell is not dividing. This packaging changes during the cell cycle at the time of division. When DNA becomes more tightly packaged it condenses into chromosomes. Each non-sex cell contains 46 chromosomes and is diploid because it possesses two sets of 23 chromosomes, each set originating from one parent. The male sperm and female egg (the sex cells) contain 23 chromosomes and are haploid because they have one set maternally or paternally derived.

Nucleic acids consist of a nitrogenous base, a 5-carbon sugar, and a phosphate group. The bases are pyrimidines and purines which differ by chemical structure. Pyrimidines are six-member rings and include: cytosine (C), thymine (T), and uracil (U). Purines are fused five and six member rings and include adenine (A) and guanine (G). (See figure 1)

Whereas C, A, and G are found in both DNA and RNA, T is only found in DNA and U is specific for RNA. A nitrogenous base bound to a five-carbon sugar is a nucleoside. The sugars of DNA and RNA are deoxyribose and ribose, respectively. The addition of a phosphate group to a nucleoside forms a nucleotide. Nucleic acids, then, are chemically linked sequences of nucleotides (See figure 2).

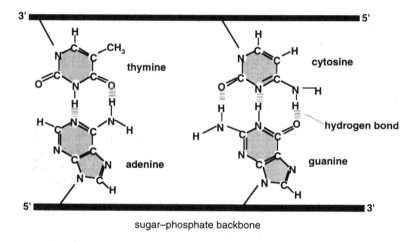

Figure 1. The four nitrogenous bases of DNA

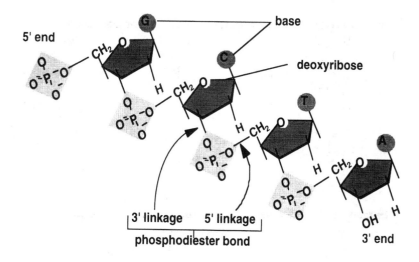

Figure 2. The chemical bonding of nucleotides

The chemistry of nucleic acids is complex and goes beyond the scope of this chapter. Some key concepts about the structure of DNA, however, are critical to a basic understanding of how DNA carries genetic information and how that information is translated into a protein chain via the genetic code.

The structure of DNA is a double helix whose backbone is composed of sugars bound to phosphates. The distance between the two polynucleotide strands (i.e., the diameter of the helix) is constant. The bases of each chain face inward with a purine always binding a pyrimidine. The "rungs" of the helix consist of complementary base pairs connected by hydrogen bonds: G bonds only with C and A only with T. (See figure 3)

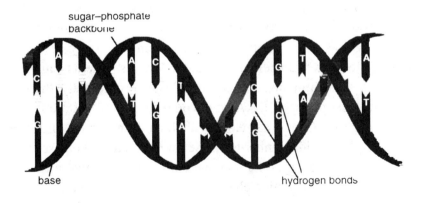

Figure 3. The double helix of DNA

The linear arrangement of nucleotides and their bases comprises the genetic "alphabet" and provides the hereditary information of DNA (i.e., the genetic code). Three successive nucleotides with their corresponding bases make up a codon. Each codon encodes one of twenty amino acids. A series of amino acids makes up a polypeptide chain or protein. Since many amino acids are specified by more than one codon the code is often referred to as degenerate. Three codons are termination signals and one is an initiation signal. In order for protein synthesis to occur, DNA must first be transcribed into RNA summarized as:[4]

$$\text{DNA} \atop \text{Replication} \xrightarrow{\text{transcription}} \text{RNA} \xrightarrow{\text{translation}} \text{Protein}$$

A gene, then, is a segment of DNA involved in producing a polypeptide chain located on a specific region or genetic loci of chromosomes.[5] It includes regions preceding and following the coding loci as well as noncoding, intervening sequences called introns located between individual coding segments called exons.[5] The human genome contains approximately three billion base pairs of DNA and codes for about 50,000 to 100,000 genes. Genes may exist in alternate forms called alleles. Since each individual inherits one set of maternal and one set of paternal chromosomes, he may have no more than two alleles for one gene. Nucleotide changes or mutations may also occur in the gene that can result in minor effects or pathological consequences. Deleting one base at the ABO locus, for instance, can change a blood type. Sickle cell anemia, caused by a single base substitution, alters the codon, replaces one amino acid for another, and results in an altered gene product (i.e., an abnormal type of hemoglobin). In a healthy population, a gene may exist in multiple alleles (e.g., the ABO blood group locus). Multiple different forms at a gene locus in a population is referred to as genetic polymorphism, the molecular basis of forensic DNA typing.[6]

Base sequences in disease states have enabled molecular biologists to mark selected areas on chromosomes in their attempt to sequence portions of the genome. This work has revealed that much of the genome consists of nucleotide sequences occurring outside of genes which are similar to introns in that they have a non-coding function. Although these non-coding sequences are often referred to as "junk DNA" and their exact purpose is not well understood, most differences in the human genome occur in these regions. These genetic polymorphisms are unique between individuals. The nucleotide sequences exist as variable numbers of tandem repeat (VNTR) sequences, each approximately 20-40 base pairs in length, repeated a different number of times in each individual. For instance, one person might have 14 repeats of a DNA segment on one chromosome and eight repeats on the other, while a second person might have 20 repeats on both.[7] Identifying these areas creates the DNA fingerprint of an individual.

Genetic polymorphism has been used in forensic science for many years. For instance, detecting variations in ABO blood group and Rh-typing system are vital to paternity cases. These nucleotide sequence variations can be detected utilizing several DNA-typing techniques. The two most common are restriction fragment length polymorphism (RFLP) analysis and PCR.

Technical Considerations

Forensic typing compares isolated DNA from biological evidence (e.g., blood, semen, tissues) found at a crime scene with DNA isolated from a known sample (usually blood) of a suspect or victim.[6] The amount of DNA isolated from a known sample can range from 1 ng/ml to 300,000 ng/ml. With recent technology, DNA can be obtained from 1 μl of blood that represents 60 ng of human genomic DNA.[7]

The most common method of DNA typing is RFLP analysis of VNTR loci, and is performed in the following manner (see figure 4).[6] First, following standard protocols, DNA is extracted and purified. Second, DNA is cut into fragments using enzymes called restriction endonucleases that recognize short sequences of DNA and cleave only at or near specific, tandemly repeated base sequences. These areas, referred to as restriction enzyme recognition sites, occur on either side of the polymorphic locus of interest. They often occur as a palindrome, a sequence of DNA that is the same when either strand is read 5' to 3'.

5' GAATTC 3'
3' CTTAAG 5'

Since the DNA fragments are of variable lengths, they are referred to as restriction fragment length polymorphisms (RFLPs). Third, these fragments are sorted based on size by electrophoresis in an agarose gel. This entails applying an electric current through a gel resulting in the smallest fragments migrating to the bottom of the gel, and the largest fragment remaining on top. Fourth, DNA is made single stranded (denatured) and a nylon membrane is placed on top of the gel. DNA is transferred to the membrane by capillary action and fixed by baking, making it accessible to a probe. Fifth, a radioactive probe specifically binds (hybridizes) to appropriate VNTR fragments by complementary base pairing. Sixth, x-ray film is placed over the membrane and the DNA profile is visualized by autoradiography.

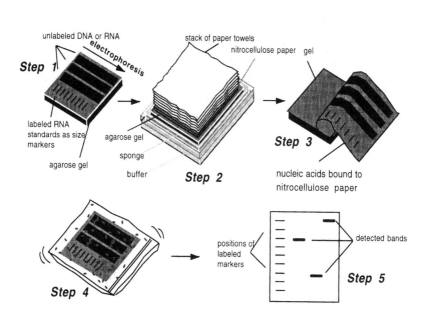

Figure 4. Detection of specific DNA molecules by Southern blotting. (Note: if single-stranded molecules of RNA are to be detected, the method is basically the same and is referred to as Northern blotting).

Step1.   Separation of nucleic acids band on size by agarose gel electrophoresis.

Steps 2 and 3. Transfer of separated nucleic acids from gel to nitrocellulose paper.

Step 4.   Hybridization with radioactive probe.

Step 5.   Autoradiograph of DNA profile.

This procedure was developed in 1975 by Dr. Southern and hence is named the "Southern blot technique."[8] Jeffreys, *et al.* adopted it for RFLP analysis and performed the first DNA fingerprinting in England in 1985.[1] The DNA banding patterns were difficult to interpret because he used probes that contained core sequences of base pairs that identified tandem repeats on many different chromosomes.[7] The following year, the so-called single-locus probe method was introduced and has become the preferred method.[6]

One problem in forensics is the acquisition of an adequate specimen for DNA extraction. Sometimes a sample is small or contaminated and yields an insufficient amount of DNA for analysis. The introduction of PCR by Kary Mullis in 1985 enabled researchers to amplify small amounts of DNA.[9,10] Indeed, PCR constitutes a major advance in molecular biology as is suggested by Dr. Mullis' Nobel Prize and has proven to be invaluable in research, the diagnosis of disease, and forensic science.

The theory behind PCR is based on certain aspects of DNA replication. An enzyme called DNA polymerase is one of the key components. As its name suggests, it functions by helping to expand a short sequence into a longer one or a polymer. DNA polymerase needs single stranded DNA that acts as a template for the synthesis of a new strand. By heating regular double stranded DNA to almost boiling, the two strands of the double helix will dissociate and become single stranded. Cooling the reaction will cause strands to reassociate (or anneal).

DNA polymerase also requires a small portion of double-stranded DNA to initiate (or "prime") synthesis. Consequently, these small portions have been referred to as primers. Each separated strand can serve as a template for synthesis as long as a primer is provided for each strand, and the reaction is cooled to cause the primers to bind. The primers are chosen to flank the region of DNA that is to be amplified. New primer binding sites are generated on each synthesized DNA strand. The reaction is reheated, the original and newly synthesized strands are separated, the reaction is recooled, primers rebind, and DNA is synthesized. This cycle is repeated many times. The desired DNA sequence lies between the primer and the net result of a PCR, after several cycles, is amplification of the specified region.

When PCR was first introduced, the reaction had to be warmed and cooled manually. A typical reaction of 32 cycles became labor intensive. The process is now completely automated with thermocyclers that contain a heating block and microprocessors. The time and temperature can be programmed for repetitive cycles of heating and cooling, alleviating manual intervention. Moreover, a special type of DNA polymerase has been discovered in bacteria living in hot springs that has an optimal temperature at 72°C and is reasonably stable at 94°C. Since this species lives in water at a temperature of 75°C it was named *Thermus aquaticus*, and its DNA polymerase was named using the first letters of its name, i.e., Taq polymerase. The optimization of PCR is also improved by Taq polymerase, since denaturation and primer extension often occur at approximately 92° and 72°, respectively.

Figure 5 illustrates the PCR reaction, but note that each cycle is repetitious and can be summarized as:

Separate strands

Anneal primers

Extend new chain with Taq polymerase

The theory and actual procedure of PCR appear deceivingly simple. It can, however, become problematic even to an experienced user. Most important, forensic specimens are often contaminated, making the extraction of pure DNA difficult. Moreover, cross contamination of DNA between two specimens, or aerosol DNA from previous reactions on one's hands at very small concentrations, can alter results. Furthermore, one must be aware of which area of DNA to analyze and how to choose appropriate primers. The reaction is extremely sensitive, requiring specific conditions and small concentrations so that one must pay very close attention to detail. Hence, there is an art to performing PCR successfully and obtaining adequate pure results, especially in the forensic setting.

In forensic diagnostics, PCR-based strategies have many advantages over RFLP analysis.[6] PCR utilizes trace amounts of DNA. 25 ng. of human DNA is usually optimal for PCR, whereas RFLP typing requires approximately 300-500 ng. PCR also generates large amounts of pure product in a shorter period of time than required by RFLP analysis. DNA degradation is less of a concern when using PCR because the reaction is

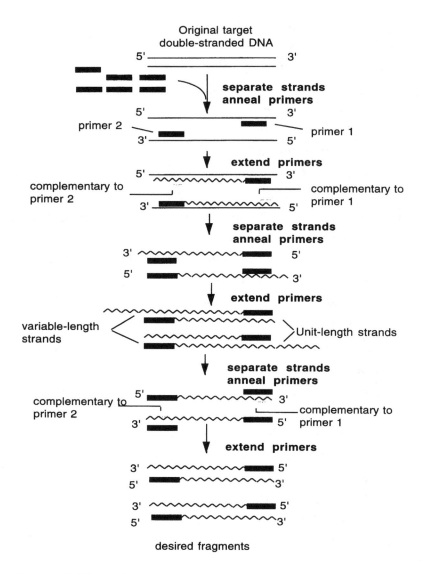

Figure 5. The polymerase chain reaction

directed at small segments. RFLP, however, requires larger samples with higher molecular weights.

After performing a DNA typing, what criteria are used to determine if two samples arose from one source? DNA testing laboratories use a two-step process. First, DNA-banding patterns are compared visually.[6] If banding patterns of a sample in question do not match a known DNA sample, an exclusion is declared and no further analysis is required. Second, a visualized match is verified by a technique called computer-assisted allele sizing.[6] The FBI and other organizations have developed special software to perform this method. Basically, the calculated sizes of an apparent match should fall within 2.5% of each other. When samples fall outside of the 2.5% window, they should be considered "nonmatching." If the DNA-banding pattern of a sample cannot be positively determined due to technical problems, the results should be considered inconclusive.[6]

Other PCR based methods that have been recently developed include: dot blots, involving a series of DNA probes to detect target sequences such as the HLA DQa locus in chromosome 6, producing a pattern of colored dots; amplified fragment length polymorphism (AMP-FLP); short tandem repeats; a system utilizing mitochondrial DNA; and digital DNA typing.[6,11]

Statistical Basis for Interpretation

Except for identical twins, no two persons have the same DNA sequence. Unique identification with DNA typing may be achieved if enough sites of variation are examined.[2] Although present DNA typing systems analyze few areas of variation, a match between two DNA patterns is strong evidence that two samples originated from the same source.[2] The interpretation of DNA typing necessitates a reliable and reproducible scientific method that estimates whether a random sample from a person matches by chance a forensic sample at sites of DNA variation. "To say that two patterns match, without providing any scientifically valid estimate. . . of the frequency with which such matches might occur by chance is meaningless."[2]

Population frequencies are often determined from theoretical models of population genetics. The multiplication rule is one method often cited and used in DNA fingerprinting. It states that the frequencies of individual alleles may be multiplied together to arrive at a frequency of the composite DNA, and is based on two broad assumptions. First, each matching allele provides statistically independent evidence. Second, the population does not contain a subpopulation with distinct allele frequencies. This implies that an individual's alleles comprise a statistically independent random selection from a common gene pool. The procedure is straightforward and has been cited elsewhere.[2] A subpopulation (e.g., those of Italian descent) would obviously violate the second assumption as well as the first because the presence of one allele in a person's genotype can alter the statistical expectations of other alleles in the genotype.[2] For example, if a particular allele at a VNTR locus has a 1% frequency in the general population and a 20%

frequency in the Italian subgroup, the frequency of homozygotes for the allele would be 1 in 10,000 (1/100 x 1/100 = 1/10,000) for the general population but 1 in 25 (1/5 x 1/5 = 1/25) for the Italian subgroup.[2]

Consequently, whether actual populations have significant substructure for the loci used in DNA typing has stimulated much debate among population geneticists. The Committee on DNA Technology in Forensic Science has decided that a population substructure may exist and provided a means for estimating population frequencies by use of the ceiling principle.[2] This involves two steps. First a ceiling frequency or an upper limit of the allele frequency that is independent of a subject's ethnic background is determined for each allele at each locus. Second, the multiplication rule is applied according to the ceiling frequencies to calculate a genotype frequency.[2]

The following recommendations have been made by the Committee:

- As a basis for the interpretation of the statistical significance of DNA typing results, the committee recommends that blood samples be obtained from 100 randomly selected persons in each of 15-20 relatively homogeneous populations; that the DNA in lymphocytes from these blood samples be used to determine the frequencies of alleles currently tested in forensic applications; and that the lymphocytes be "immortalized" and preserved as a reference standard for determination of allele frequencies in tests applied in different laboratories or developed in the future. The collection of samples and their study should be overseen by a National Committee on Forensic DNA Typing.

• In the interval (which should be short) while the reference blood samples are being collected, the significance of the findings of multilocus DNA typing should be presented in two ways: (1) If no match is found with any sample in a total databank of N persons (as will usually be the case), that should be stated, thus indicating the rarity of a random match. (2) In applying the multiplication rule, the 95% upper confidence limit of the frequency of each allele should be calculated for separate U.S. "racial" groups and the highest of these values or 10% (whichever is the larger) should be used. Data on at least three major "races" (e.g., Caucasians, blacks, Hispanics, Asians, and Native Americans) should be analyzed.

• Any population databank used to support DNA typing should be openly available for scientific inspection by parties to a legal case and by the scientific community.

• Laboratory error rates should be measured with appropriate proficiency tests and should play a role in the interpretation of results of forensic DNA typing.[2]

It should be noted that recently the NRC has withdrawn the recommendation of a ceiling principle. Presently, the NRC recommends a more flexible approach in which odds are calculated on the frequency at which specific DNA markers occur in particular ethnic groups.[12] Details on population genetics and the Hardy-Weinberg Equilibrium are covered elsewhere.[3,6,13]

Concluding Remarks

Regardless of whether DNA typing is used for paternity or criminal cases, a body is almost always available in addition to an eyewitness or confession from the accused. Although there have been several successfully prosecuted murder cases in which a victim's body was not discovered, very few cases exist in which there was no eyewitness or confession and DNA played an integral part.[14]

One landmark case, Missouri vs. Davis, involved a man accused of killing his wife after she had been missing for approximately two years. The case focused on an automobile proved to be owned by the missing woman and her husband. Fragments of bone, glass, shotgun pellets, and dried blood were found in the car. Samples of the dried blood and specimens were obtained from the defendant and his children. Four single-locus probes were used to obtain DNA fingerprints. One child's blood contained two bands corresponding to those from blood in the car and four bands similar to those of the defendant. The second child's blood had four bands matching those from blood in the car and three matching the defendant. It was concluded that the blood from the car came from the mother of these two children and the likelihood that it came from anyone other than the defendant's wife was one in 22 billion. An additional unique aspect to the evidence was that conventional DNA matching could not occur because a blood sample was unavailable from the deceased. Moreover, paternity testing, i.e., comparing the unknown sample to the DNA of the missing woman's parents, could not be performed because the woman was adopted and her biological parents were unknown.

This case, in part, exemplifies the power of DNA evidence. Although the defense attorney tried to convince the jury that they could never be completely certain that the defendant's wife was dead since a body was not discovered, the jury found him guilty and sentenced him to death.[14] Obviously, the DNA evidence was irrefutable, leaving the defense unable to criticize its methodology or statistical analysis.

The case can also be used as an introduction to some legal considerations concerning forensic DNA testing. DNA fingerprinting, as we have seen, has two major components: DNA analysis for matching purposes, and the statistical analysis to determine the probability that a presumptive match would occur by chance alone. When DNA typing was first introduced into forensic science, molecular biology was making great advances in diagnosing diseases and the Human Genome Project was starting to map our entire genetic makeup. Many research facilities were also performing molecular analysis and no standards existed for laboratories to perform molecular diagnostics in the clinical setting. With the introduction of PCR, DNA fingerprinting appeared to be a simple method for those set up for molecular diagnostics. Consequently, results from one lab could not easily be reproduced, the purity of data was questionable because of the likelihood of contamination, and the credibility of a facility could often easily be destroyed. Moreover, some criticized the statistics being applied asking, for instance, was the Hardy–Weinberg law used?; is a probability such as one in 100,000 accurate when certain ethnic groups were included in a population?; should a criminal subpopulation be used?; is the multiplication rule valid? By the time of the NRC report, Cellmark laboratory, the FBI, and a few other facilities had established credibility in the forensic community so that the technical aspect of DNA fingerprinting could not be easily attacked. After publication of the report with recommendations and standards, even the statistics left little room for criticism.

In conversations with prosecuting attorneys and expert witnesses, several issues remain for a defense attorney to criticize DNA evidence. Above all, it is most important to remember that a defense attorney's obligation is to ensure that all evidence is sound. With DNA testing, this means to ensure that it was properly performed. Consequently, the defense will scrutinize a case with the intent to expose or capitalize upon any weakness such as a weak chain of custody. Once that is determined, then he will challenge the DNA evidence and the methodology employed. Some common areas to attack are:

laboratory accreditation and quality control; adherence to protocols, FBI guidelines, or NRC recommendations; past improprieties such as failing a laboratory inspection or association with unreliable PCR-based testing; methods to assure against contamination; data base used for statistical analysis; and as seen in the O.J. Simpson trial, the possibility of planting or tampering with evidence. We are reminded, however, of Dr. Lander's comment in the introduction, that if the practiced standards in the field of forensic DNA typing have been followed, the accuracy cannot be repudiated.

References:

1. Jeffreys AJ, Thein SL, Wilson V: Individual specific "fingerprints" of human DNA. Nature 316:76-79, 1985.
2. National Research Council. "DNA Technology in Forensic Science," Washington, DC, National Academy Press, 1992.
3. Lander ES, Budowle B: DNA fingerprinting dispute laid to rest. Nature 371:735-738, 1994.
4. Watson JD, Gilman M, Witkowski J, Zoller M: "Recombinant DNA," 2nd ed. New York, WH Freeman and Co, 1992.
5. Lewin B: "Genes V," New York, Oxford University Press, 1994.
6. Lee HC, Ladd C, Bourke MT, Pagliaro E, Tirnady F.: DNA typing in forensic science. The American Journal of Forensic Medicine and Pathology 15:269-282, 1994.

7. Zumwalt RE: Application of molecular biology to forensic pathology. Human Pathology 20:303-307, 1989.

8. Southern EM: Detection of specific sequences among DNA fragments separated by gel electrophoresis. J Mol Biol. 98:503-517, 1975.

9. Mullis KB, Faloona FA, Scharf SJ, Saiki RK, Erlich HA, Arnheim N: Specific enzymatic amplification of DNA in vitro: the polymerase chain reaction. Cold Spring Harbor Symp. Quant. Biol. 51:263-273, 1986.

10. Saiki R, Scharf S, Faloona F, Mullis KB, Horn GT, Erlich HA, Arnheim N: Enzymatic amplification of ß-globin genomic sequences and restriction site analysis for diagnosis of sickle cell anemia. Science 230:1350-1354, 1985.

11. Weedn VW: Forensic DNA tests. In Farkas DH (ed): "DNA Technology," Clinics in Laboratory Medicine 16:187-196,1996.

12. Academy's about-face on forensic DNA. Science 272: 803, 1996.

13. Alberts B, Bray D, Lewis J, Raff M, Roberts K, Watson JD: "Molecular Biology of the Cell," 3rd Ed. New York: Garland Publishing, Inc., 1994.

14. Dix JD, Stout SD, Mosley J: Bones, blood, pellets, glass and no body. Journal of Forensic Sciences 36:949-952,1991.

15. Housman DE: DNA on trial — the molecular basis of DNA fingerprinting. The New England Journal of Medicine 332:534-535, 1995.

16. Weir BS: DNA statistics in the Simpson matter. Nature Genetics 11:365-368, 1995.

PART IV

Commonly Asked Questions

1. *How long was he dead prior to discovery?*

Determination of the time of death is usually an inexact science. Every pathologist should only attempt an estimation using a variety of signs from both the body and scene. Body rigidity and temperature, settling blood, and stomach contents are some signs that can be obtained from a body. A scene must be thoroughly analyzed for clues and one should ask questions such as: Are the lights on or off? Has the mail been picked up? Are major appliances in use? What is the environmental temperature? This information can help an examiner formulate an impression and compare it to witnessed accounts.

Environmental temperature is the most important factor in determining the postmortem interval. The hotter a climate, the faster a body stiffens and decomposes. Most pathologists rely on body temperature alone because they do not know the temperature at a scene. A pathologist is at a disadvantage when a body is placed in a refrigerator prior to an autopsy or the decedent is transported over long distances. There may be marked temperature variation at a scene because doors and windows may be closed or opened after a body is discovered. If body temperature at a scene is important, the scene investigator should make two measurements (usually rectal) before a body is moved.

Stomach contents can also be used to estimate the time of death. Food usually passes through the stomach within a few hours. An examiner, however, should be careful when giving a time frame because excitement or stress may either increase or retard emptying time.

There are rare occasions in which the precise time of death can be ascertained. One instance is by a witness who may know the time within a few minutes. If a witness states that he observed a death, the story needs to be substantiated by a pathologist via information obtained from both an examination of the body and a scene investigation. All eyewitness accounts should be verified. A second way of establishing the precise time of death is by using a decedent's watch which may break at the time of injury. Even in this rare case, the signs of death from the body and scene should be taken into account.

Attorneys usually want an expert witness to give a time of death during testimony. When they do not receive an exact time a typical follow-up question is "Doctor, can you give me a range?" A consulting pathologist should be careful in this instance. An acceptable range may be provided if all the facts of a case, including scene and body descriptions, are known. It is usually easier for a well-trained pathologist to give a range if he performed an autopsy and had accessible scene information. A consultant rarely has all the information and often relies on what others have reported since he usually neither performed the autopsy nor went to the scene. A consultant can give an opinion and occasionally may possess as much information as the pathologist who performed the autopsy. A pathologist often examines the body hours after it arrives at the morgue. The body may have been examined at the scene by an investigator who may not have been adequately trained and the pathologist must rely on this investigator's expertise.

Most pathologists prefer giving an opinion as to whether the time of death was consistent with the history or the witness's statement. A pathologist should testify to the validity of a witness's account.

2. *How long did he live after he was injured?*

Very few victims of trauma die immediately after receiving their injuries. Even gunshot wounds to the heart or brain may not cause instant death. Every pathologist can recount an anecdote of a person who received such injuries and survived longer than thought possible. For example, a man whose heart was penetrated with a stab wound ran to his car, drove across a small town to the emergency room, ran through the door, and then expired. No one would have expected him to live for this period and run after sustaining such serious injuries.

In these types of deaths, it is important to know which organ was injured, as well as the type of injury that organ received. A gunshot wound to the head, for example, may or may not cause significant brain injury. A bullet straight through the side of the head, as in a typical suicide gunshot wound, renders an individual unconscious immediately after the gun is fired because the bullet passes through vital brain structures. If the bullet does not directly enter the brain, an individual may remain conscious for a longer period since fewer important areas would be damaged. Not all individuals react the same way to similar gunshot wounds. The same gunshot wound may also cause slightly different damages to the brain because of differences in bullet energy.

A pathologist should be able to estimate how long a person survived after an injury and his physical capability. A fatal gunshot wound may not quickly incapacitate a person. A victim may continue to be the aggressor even after a gunshot wound to the heart. An attorney (state or defense) needs to know some of these answers to make a case, verify a witness's credibility, or pursue a particular line of defense.

A person may become unconscious after receiving a nonfatal injury and he may then be killed by another type of injury. An estimation of a victim's response to a particular injury is difficult for a pathologist because individuals respond to injuries differently. If two people receive the same blow to the head, one may become unconscious and the other may not. An unconscious person may then die from complications of brain swelling or some other means. A victim may also be assaulted by two people and receive two injuries capable of causing death. The second injury, however, would probably be the cause of death if a pathologist could be certain that the victim remained alive after receiving the first injury.

Attorneys are occasionally concerned with the actual moment of a person's death. They may be interested in exactly when the heart stopped beating or when the brain ceased to function. Pathologists rarely are concerned with the exact time of death because they would have no way of knowing the exact moment a heart stops beating or a brain ceases to have electrical activity. A pathologist usually relies on a witness's account of the time of death, especially if the witness is an emergency room physician who pronounced the individual dead.

3. How long does it take to strangle someone?

Strangulation causes death by asphyxia or lack of oxygen to the brain by compressing the larynx or trachea, or by significantly slowing blood flow to the brain. Death may also occur if blood flow cannot return to the heart. Airway compression or interference with blood flow must be caused by a second party for a death to be called a strangulation. An assailant can accomplish this by using his hands or some other object. If his hands are used, a pathologist refers to the death as a manual throttling; if another object is used, the death is referred to as a ligature strangulation. A mark left on the neck from a ligature strangulation will usually be a straight line abrasion with possible contusions. The neck in a throttling case, however, will have mostly bruising or abrasions and fingernail marks appearing as small cuts.

A victim may be rendered unconscious within a few seconds if a choke hold is used. Pressure is applied to both sides of the neck simultaneously. The assailant grabs the victim with one arm from behind and squeezes. The pressure may be continued until the person dies or stopped causing unconsciousness. If a choke hold is used to cause death, there may be no external signs because the force is applied evenly over a large area so that bruising does not occur. There may be, however, other injuries to the neck if a person was killed by manual throttling or a ligature.

Death by ligature or manual throttling may cause few significant injuries to the neck. The amount of damage to the extreme or internal aspect of the neck does not indicate how long pressure was applied or how long a person lived. A person who is incapable of putting up any kind of fight may have very few or no injuries. Faint external bruises and few signs of blood in the internal tissues may be apparent. This is especially true for infants and the elderly. A baby or comatose adult who is suffocated may have neither external nor internal signs of trauma. Either individual may be killed by placing a pillow, hand, or other object over the nose and mouth leaving no signs of trauma. If there is no struggle, injuries cannot occur.

4. *How old are the bruises?*

The answer to this question is difficult for both attorney and pathologist. An attorney, for instance, needs to know if bruises occurred at the time of an alleged trauma, such as during a homicide or a sexual assault. Too often, however, there is no direct answer.

One of the main problems in the development of bruises is individual variation. A typical bruise goes through a series of color changes from red, red-blue, blue, blue-green, or brown to yellow before it fades. Unfortunately, not all bruises go through the same series of color changes and recent ones have brown or yellow mixed in with an overall red or blue color. Some people bruise more easily than others. This is especially true in the elderly because their skin and blood vessels are more fragile.

The time a body takes to rid itself of a bruise varies from individual to individual. Most people take 2-3 weeks to heal a bruise while some may take more than a month. The time it takes for bruises to become evident is also variable and has to do with the location of a damaged body part and the depth of torn blood vessels within soft tissues. If an injury is deep, a bruise may not become apparent for a day or more, while a superficial injury may be noticeable within minutes or hours.

If a person lives after receiving an injury, the size and color of a bruise may be different than if a person died suddenly after a traumatic event. If injured blood vessels continue to bleed because the heart is still pumping, a bruise will be larger because more blood has seeped into tissues. If a person sustained massive injuries, including the rupture of a major blood vessel, and his heart suddenly ceased to pump, then the bruises will be faint because less blood is getting to smaller vessels.

A pathologist may take a bruised piece of skin and process it for microscopic examination in order to view a body's response to an injury. The body's white blood cells clean up injured cells and assist in scar formation. White blood cells can be seen microscopically approximately one half hour after the initial injury. After a few days cells which will later form scar tissue can be seen. If microscopic sections are taken, they should be obtained form the edge of the bruise since the middle portion contains more blood and takes longer to heal. The edge provides the best estimate of the age of a bruise. Unfortunately, neither color nor microscopy allows a pathologist to render an opinion with certainty.

5. *How much force did it take to cause the injury?*

Many attorneys ask about the severity of a blow that caused the injury. A pathologist usually cannot tell exactly how much force was applied because there is no way to measure the amount necessary to break a bone or cause a bruise. Studies of forces causing fractures or bruises are difficult since human models have been inadequate. Some pathologists may provide an anecdote of how much pressure it took by recounting a case of known circumstances. If pressed, some pathologist may give an answer in foot pounds of pressure (a standard measure of energy) which is usually meaningless.

6. *What was the decedent capable of doing after he was injured?*

See question #2.

7. *Were the injuries caused by a man or a woman?*

There is no way to determine whether a man or woman caused an injury since both are capable of causing bruises or severe traumatic injuries. Fingermark contusions (bruises) may be present on the extremities of women and they are strong enough to bruise another's arm. Regardless of the size of a bruise, a positive match with a suspect cannot be made. Men more commonly cause an inordinate number of stab wounds, gunshot wounds, or numerous blunt impact injuries. Men inflict more severe and greater numbers of injuries, but this may also be due to the fact that they are more involved in homicides, especially those associated with drugs and sex. Moreover, men are typically are involved in greater trauma than women who usually need heavier weapons to cause severe injury. This is a common question in a case of child abuse when a suspect may be either an adult man or woman.

8. *What type of weapon caused these injuries?*

This question usually occurs in cases of blunt trauma where there are contusions, abrasions, and lacerations of the skin. Rarely is the question associated with a death due to a gunshot wound or a sharp instrument. An incised wound may be confused with a laceration but a forensic pathologist is usually able to differentiate. A cutting injury incises skin and tissues cleanly through to the bottom of the wound. A laceration may have strands of tissue bridging from one side of a wound to the other.

A weapon such as a hammer tends to leave distinct marks on the skin, especially in areas where bone is close to the surface. Hammer marks are usually not difficult to determine in the skull since the skin will have semicircular abrasions or lacerations, and the skull will commonly fracture in a similar semicircular fashion. These patterns are more readily apparent because of the weight of the hammer head in such a concentrated area.

Other objects such as clubs do not leave easily recognizable patterns because the weight of a club is distributed over a wide area. Thin, heavy weapons such as a tire iron or a fire poker may leave linear marks with pale centers; thin light weapons such as a coat hanger or belt also leave easily recognizable patterns. Bumpers, headlights, and other parts of a vehicle may leave patterns due to the tremendous force which occurs when a vehicle strikes a body. In a small percentage of blunt trauma cases an object can be determined with certainty.

9. Were these antemortem or postmortem injuries?

A definitive answer as to whether or not the injuries occurred postmortem or antemortem may be impossible to give. An examiner makes a determination based on the amount of blood in the soft tissues or the presence of blood on the edges of the external wounds. A decedent's skin can be torn and scraped after death, but there is usually very little bleeding in the surrounding tissues. A considerable amount of blood, however, may seep into surrounding tissues if a body is in a dependent position. Cutting injuries may have associated crushing of tissues which, if present, means a person was alive when the injury occurred. This question is also commonly asked when there has been a sexual assault. Tears of vaginal or rectal tissue or cutting injuries can occur during a sexual assault and after death.

Postmortem scrapes tend to be dry and brown with no bleeding around the edges. This is especially true when a dead body has been dragged. An examiner will make multiple cuts into the body areas when he is uncertain if the injuries are postmortem or not. The purpose of this procedure is to look for blood in soft tissues beneath the skin. If blood is present he knows a decedent was alive when injured.

10. *What type of knife caused the injury?*

There are always many questions concerning the type of weapon used to stab or cut a person. Most sharp instruments such as scissors, knives, or razors will cause a cutting injury and there is no way to differentiate which one was used. Occasionally, a very sharp instrument like a razor will leave a cleaner, more even edge to a cut than a dull knife. If a weapon has a serrated edge, and is not a knife, an evaluation might be somewhat easier, but the actual weapon can never be matched with certainty. An instrument with a short blade will not usually cause a very deep wound inside the body.

Stab wounds are not usually as difficult to evaluate as incised wounds. A blade 6 inches long can cause a 7 inch deep wound because skin and tissue collapse under the force of the thrust. After the weapon is withdrawn, tissue and skin return to their original position. Skin elasticity also causes wounds to take different shapes than that of a blade. A 1 inch wide blade may cause a slightly smaller opening such as 15/16 or 7/8 inch. A gaping wound may also open wider than the size of the blade.

Stab wounds are described by the length and depth of a cut. The corners or angles of an external wound are evaluated as to their sharpness or bluntness. If one angle is sharp and the other almost flat then a commercially made knife, similar to a standard pocket knife, was used. It is uncommon to find both angles very sharp. Weapons found in prisons may cause wounds having sharp angles, but not as sharp as if commercially made instruments were used. Sometimes hand-sharpened weapons will have fairly dull edges making evaluation very difficult, especially if the wound is dry.

An external wound is commonly longer than the width of a blade. An external wound may also be longer than the blade size if the victim moves during a stabbing. There may be trailing edges of a wound which are very shallow or a wound may be angled or V-shaped. The same knife may cause different appearing external wounds and different internal depths.

A blade with a certain length can cause a deeper or longer wound in a body because tissues can easily collapse. The angles of a weapon can also be evaluated internally when a weapon passes through or into an organ. This can be very helpful when an external wound has dried.

A knife with a blade 1 inch wide and 6 inches long can cause a 2-inch external wound and an 8-inch internal wound. The same knife, however, could not cause a wound 6 inches deep with an external wound of only 5/8 inch because the blade at that depth is 1 inch wide. An external wound cannot be significantly smaller in length than the width of the blade.

Abrasions or contusions occur rarely at the edges of a knife wound. The hilt of a knife may uncommonly damage skin during a thrust.

Since an examination of a wound cannot provide a match to a weapon, other information is needed such as analyzing blood on a weapon and matching it to a victim, or discovering a broken tip from a blade and matching it to a suspected weapon.

11. *Was more than one knife used?*

As discussed in question #10, a knife can cause a variety of cutting and stabbing wounds. Both internal and external wounds can vary by inches. It is much more difficult to distinguish between two knives than between a knife and a chopping instrument. The best chance an examiner has is if numerous stab wounds are present since they are the best indicators of the width and length of the blade. The more stab wounds, the better chance an examiner has of determining if more than one knife was used. Most people are killed with one weapon.

12. *Who was the driver?*

This question is asked when there is more than one occupant in a vehicle and both are ejected or end up in unusual positions during an accident. When an accident occurs, occupants will have injuries as if they traveled in the direction of the impact. For example, a head-on collision at the left front of a vehicle will cause all occupants to move toward the left upon impact. If no occupants are ejected, then there will be little difficulty deciding who was driving because a driver usually remains behind the wheel. Occasionally, a passenger and driver may trade places in a complicated crash, such as when a vehicle rolls over multiple times.

If all occupants are ejected and die, they need to be examined because certain points of impact within a vehicle cause specific injuries. The side windows of automobiles are tempered glass

141

which breaks into numerous cubes and rectangles and cause a "dicing" abrasion characteristically shaped with right angles. The marks may be either abrasions or shallow skin cuts. A driver of a vehicle will commonly have these dicing abrasions on the left side of his face or on the left shoulder, whereas a front seat passenger will have them on the right side of the body. An accident involving a windshield does not result in dicing injuries since it is not made of tempered glass. A windshield is laminated in two layers and, upon impact, the glass does not shatter like the side windows but commonly remains intact.

Since occupants travel in the direction of impact, their bodies typically have injuries caused by other parts of a car's interior. In order to determine who was driving, an examiner looks for chest injuries from a steering wheel or lower extremity fractures due to braking or accelerating. Therefore, a car's damaged interior must be compared to the bodily injuries. Blood, hair, and other body tissues may be deposited within a car. These specimens can be compared to those obtained during a postmortem examination.

If all occupants are ejected from a car and there are no injuries, the problem of deciding who was driving becomes more difficult to solve. The accident may need to be reconstructed by an expert, usually a law enforcement official or private consultant. Prior to finding a consultant, a pathologist should review the accident report. Many reports are good enough to use without consulting another expert. If an expert is consulted, he should contact the pathologist to review their findings. Both parties should be able to work together to arrive at a solution.

13. *How close was the gun to the victim when it was fired?*

This is determined by the presence or absence of gunpowder on the body or clothing. When a gun is fired, propellant or gunpowder exits as unburned and burning particles. Completely burned particles, called fouling or smoke, are the lightest and do not travel more than a foot. If a victim is less than a foot away, smoke will be deposited on a victim's clothing or skin. Heavier particles travel approximately three feet or less with a few flakes traveling a greater distance.

Smoke deposited on the skin can be easily washed off. Heavier particles, however, will embed in the skin and cannot be removed. Heavier particles embedded or abrading in skin are called "tattooing" or "stippling." At a distance of less than one foot, both fouling and tattooing are present and are indicative of a close range gunshot wound. At a distance of greater than one foot, only tattooing is present and is representative of an intermediate wound. A distant wound occurs when there is no gunpowder present, meaning a gun was held at least three feet away from a body when fired.

A gun held firmly against skin when fired will cause gunpowder to travel into a wound. Gunpowder is not found around wound edges unless a gun is loosely held next to skin. A wound in which the weapon is held firmly against skin when fired is called a tight contact wound. If a gun is loosely held next to skin and some powder is deposited on the edges of a wound, it is referred to as a loose contact wound. Tight and loose contact gunshot wounds are typically seen in suicides and execution style murders.

143

14. *What was the sequence of gunshot wounds?*

The sequence of gunshot wounds cannot be determined in many cases. Proper description and recording of the location and direction of wound tracks are important. The wounds are compared to a witness's or an assailant's account of what happened, and a pathologist decides if their stories coincide with the wounds. For example, a shot to the back may injure the spinal cord and cause a victim to become paralyzed. All shots following the first will have to match the circumstances of a man who is paralyzed. Finding bullets under a victim on the ground indicate that a person was already down when shot. This finding also helps determine at which point in the sequence a victim was actually hit.

The skull is often fractured after a gunshot wound to the head. A second shot to the head will cause more fractures. If the fracture line from the second shot runs into one from the first the fracture line stops. Unfortunately, this is an infrequent occurrence even though it can be quite useful.

15. *Can a pathologist tell the difference between a SIDS death and a suffocation homicide?*

A cause of death is not found in SIDS (Sudden Infant Death Syndrome). An autopsy is negative, except for minor diseases or postmortem artifacts from insects. Despite numerous research attempting to evaluate the etiology, the cause of death in these children is still unknown. One of the latest theories is that these children have a problem breathing when they sleep called sleep apnea. Not all researchers believe this is the cause.

Coupled with a negative autopsy is an unremarkable scene investigation. The place where a baby is discovered must be thoroughly investigated to rule out other causes of death. In fact, there should not be a ruling of SIDS unless both an autopsy and scene investigation are performed.

A baby can be easily suffocated by placing a hand or some other object over his face and nose. Since a baby is unable to defend himself there is little struggle, few if any injuries, and a negative autopsy. Therefore, a pathologist cannot distinguish between SIDS and a suffocation homicide by an autopsy. If there are no injuries, the only way to tell if a crime was committed is by an investigation.

16. *How can one tell if a person drowned?*

There is no specific test or method to determine conclusively that a person drowned. The only way a death by drowning can be proven is to have a reliable witness testify (or document) what happened. There is no such thing as proof of drowning because an examiner discovered water in the lungs. "Wet" lungs may or may not be present in a drowning death. Drowning is a diagnosis of exclusion and the autopsy is usually negative. The circumstances surrounding a death should suggest that a decedent drowned. A negative autopsy in a person discovered dead on land does not suggest drowning. A victim should be found in water or his clothes must be wet.

17. *Did the decedent fall down the stairs or did someone hit him in the head?*

Most people who die after a fall have experienced head trauma. When someone falls and strikes his head there are specific injuries to the brain which help determine falling as a cause of death. A pathologist examines the skull for point of impact and the brain for bruises. If a head is moving and strikes a stationary object there will be a brain injury opposite the site of impact called a contrecoup contusion. For example, if a man slips on a rug, falls and strikes the back of his head, there will be an anterior injury without a posterior one. If a head is stationary and then struck, the injury to the brain will be different than that of a fall and is called a coup contusion of the brain. If a man strikes another with a hammer, for instance, on the right side of the head, the brain injury will be directly beneath the point of impact.

Multiple injuries to one side of the head indicate that a decedent probably did not fall. It is difficult to fall down stairs and receive five or more lacerations to the same side of the head and in no other location. It is impossible to tell the difference between a fall or a push down a flight of stairs. A victim will receive the same injuries in either case.

18. *The driver had a 0.125 grams % blood alcohol. Was he drunk at the time of the accident?*

This driver would be considered legally intoxicated at the time the blood specimen was taken if the specimen was obtained correctly and testing was performed appropriately. An alcohol concentration measured after an accident only reveals that alcohol had been ingested at the time of measurement. The value does not indicate how much alcohol was in the system at the time of the accident or whether the alcohol content in the system was increasing, decreasing, or stabilizing.

A 150 lb. man can absorb about an ounce of alcohol (80 proof) within an hour and have a blood alcohol concentration of approximately 0.015-0.02 grams %. This driver had the equivalent of at least 6 ounces of alcohol in his system at the time he was tested. One ounce of 80 proof is equal to approximately a 12 ounce can of 6% beer, or an 8 ounce glass of wine. Once alcohol is totally absorbed, most of it is eliminated in an hour. Not all alcoholic beverages are absorbed at the same rate, especially when a drinker is also eating which inhibits alcohol absorption. These slight differences in absorption rarely present a problem when determining whether or not a driver was drunk at the time of an accident.

If a driver had numerous drinks within a couple of hours prior to an accident, his body might still be absorbing alcohol at the time of an accident. A driver might not become legally intoxicated until some time after the accident. If he stopped drinking for a considerable amount of time before an accident, then his blood alcohol would be decreasing or stabilizing by the time it was measured. He may or may not have been at the legal limit at the time of the accident. Occasionally, people drink after an accident and before they are found by the police. In this circumstance they may not have been legally drunk at the time of the accident, but are by the time they are tested.

147

The best method for determining what is happening to alcohol in the system is to take more than one measurement to evaluate whether a driver's alcohol content is increasing or decreasing. This gives a better indication as to what was happening during the accident. The most important information is the time of a driver's last drink and his total consumption.

PART V
Cases

1. *Cause, Mechanism, and Manner*
Case 1

A 25 year old man was shot in the abdomen with a handgun. He was taken to the hospital where he underwent an emergency exploratory laparotomy. All life-threatening injuries were repaired. His postoperative course, however, was complicated by peritonitis which led to sepsis and eventually death two weeks after surgery. An autopsy revealed an extensive abdominal infection. The medical examiner ruled the cause of death as a gunshot wound to the abdomen and the manner of death as a homicide.

During the trial, the pathologist was questioned about the cause of death. The pathologist reiterated his opinion that the decedent died from a gunshot wound. A fierce cross-examination followed. The defense attorney contended the man died as a result of an abdominal infection. Consequently, it was the physician, not his client, who was to blame for the death. Who should the jury believe? Would the victim have died if the infection had been discovered sooner? Should the physician be responsible for the man's death?

Case 2

A woman in her seventies was walking to a grocery store. An assailant pushed her onto the sidewalk as he grabbed her purse. She was apparently unharmed but obviously shaken by the experience. Within 10 to 15 minutes she developed shortness of breath, increased chest pain and was taken to a nearby emergency room. During her evaluation she developed an arrhythmia and died. An autopsy revealed severe atherosclerotic disease in all coronary arteries and numerous infarcts of the left ventricle. There were no signs of injury from the fall. The medical examiner ruled the cause and manner of her death as heart disease and homicide, respectively.

During the trial, the defense attorney disagreed with the cause and manner of death. He stated this was not a homicide because the woman died of heart disease, and the fall to the sidewalk caused by his client was not a contributing factor. Was the pathologist correct? Should he have called the death a homicide? Did the man who took her purse actually cause her death?

Case Discussion
Case 1

This man died as a result of a gunshot wound to the abdomen and the manner of death was homicide. It was a life-threatening injury which would have caused his death within hours if he had not been treated. A well-recognized risk of abdominal surgery is peritonitis. If he had been admitted with a nonlethal injury, and the physician made an error in judgement which caused his death, then the manner of death would have been an accident, not homicide. In this case, however, the pathologist correctly stated that the sequence of events was continuous from the time the man was shot until he died.

Case 2

This case is more complex than Case 1. The manner, not the cause, of this woman's death is in dispute. Since there was no significant trauma, the cause of death had to be the heart disease. Even the defense attorney agreed with this interpretation. He was more concerned with the sequence of events and how the pathologist believed the robbery was directly related to the death.

There was only a 10-15 minute interval from the time the woman was knocked to the ground to when she experienced signs and symptoms of a heart attack or angina. Since the time period was short, the pathologist believed that the woman was still under stress and correctly interpreted the manner of her death as a homicide. The longer the time frame, however, between the incident and heart attack, the more difficult it would be to make this interpretation. If, for example, the woman had gone home, had not been seen for a few hours, and then complained of chest pain, the same interpretation could not have been made. She would have been unwitnessed during that time and some other incident could have triggered a fatal arrhythmia. Consequently, in such a situation, her death could not be ruled a homicide.

2. *Time of Death, Decomposition, and Identification*
Case

On a hot August day, the body of an elderly man was discovered in a ditch next to a country road. He was lying supine dressed in overalls, a short-sleeved work shirt, and socks without shoes. His abdomen and legs were covered by a blanket. There was marked maggot infestation of the head and neck, partially obscuring a posterior scalp defect, and a ligature around his neck. The skin of the upper chest, neck, and head was markedly darkened. The rest of the body was not decomposed. There was no apparent blood on the ground surrounding the victim.

The scalp defect was a four inch gaping laceration with no underlying bone or brain injury. The ligature was a small towel tightly compressing the neck and knotted in the back. There was no rigor mortis and livor mortis was posterior. Stomach contents revealed fragments of sausage pieces, brown liquid, and white semi-solid food particles. At least ten maggots were saved in a container of alcohol. A diagnosis of ligature strangulation was rendered and the death was ruled a homicide.

The next day a deputy sheriff called the pathologist to asked about the time of death. The deputy was holding a man in custody who had been seen with the decedent two days before the body was discovered. The suspect claimed that he was out of town the day before the man was found dead. The suspect had a good motive for the murder because of a soured business deal with the victim. Prior to making a formal arrest, the officer needed to make sure the postmortem interval was consistent with two days. What should the pathologist say about the postmortem interval in this case?

Case Discussion
Case

One of the most frequently asked questions during death investigation concerns the time of death. Unfortunately, determining the exact time of death from an examination of a body is impossible. Numerous findings must be interpreted to give a reasonable estimation of the postmortem interval. In this particular case, the time of death was key to the arrest because the suspect had an alibi a day before the body was discovered.

In this case, differential decomposition occurred because a head injury caused an open wound. Blood is an excellent source for maggot proliferation, which accelerated the decompositional changes in the head. Since the rest of the body had not decomposed, an estimation of the postmortem interval was made by evaluating the area of least decomposition.

Environmental temperature is the most important factor in determining the rate of decompositional change after death. The decompositional changes in the head and the lack of rigor mortis could occur in 10 to 20 hours in above 90° temperatures. Therefore, in this case the postmortem interval had to be less than 24 hours.

The decedent's stomach contained pieces of sausage, brown liquid, and white food particles suggestive of breakfast foods. If he normally ate these foods only in the morning then he probably ate breakfast on the day of his death. Relatives and friends should be contacted to discover a decedent's eating habits to help determine the time of the day he was killed.

Maggot samples were not sent to an entomologist for study because the postmortem interval was sufficiently narrow making this specialized study unnecessary.

The above discussion suggests the decedent died the day before his body was discovered. Therefore, the suspect with the strong alibi did not commit the murder, and investigators need to renew their search for the killer.

153

3. *Sudden Natural Death*

Case 1

A 36-year old man was found dead at 8:30 a.m. in his bathroom, lying on his left side with nose pressed to the floor and legs bent toward the right. There was blood on the linoleum, beneath his head, associated with a laceration to the posterior scalp. He was dressed in night clothes and his body was cold and stiff. A neighbor saw a woman quickly leave the apartment and notified the superintendent who then found the body. The apartment was neat and clean except for some blood on the bed sheets. The scene did not appear as if a homicide was committed, but the medical examiner and police decided that the death should be investigated. The woman who hastily left the apartment was found. She stated that the decedent was already dead when she awoke and the blood on the bed was menstrual.

During the autopsy, the pathologist detected an enlarged, thin-walled heart with minimal triple vessel coronary artery disease and no signs of a previous heart attack. The laceration to the scalp did not extend to the skull and there were no cerebral injuries. A drug screen was positive for marijuana and a blood alcohol was 0.12 grams %. The woman's story appeared to be substantiated and his death was attributed to atherosclerotic heart disease. Was the pathologist in error? Did head trauma and/or drugs contribute to the cause of this man's death?

Case 2

The body of a partially skeletonized elderly woman was discovered lying in the basement of an abandoned building during June. She was fully clothed and next to her body were assorted bags filled with old clothes and a few pairs of shoes. In the area was an old mattress, a chair, and a makeshift stove. There were no drugs and no indications of foul play.

Closer examination revealed that portions of the face and extremities had been eaten by animals so the body was not as skeletonized as previously thought. The internal organs were intact and the brain was liquified. A complete autopsy failed to reveal any diseases or traumatic injuries and a drug screen was negative except for a trace amount of Dilantin. How should the medical examiner rule the cause and manner of death?

Case Discussion
Case 1

Initially, this case would seem suspicious because there was blood in the bed and a woman was observed fleeing the scene. A thorough scene investigation, however, revealed nothing particularly suspicious. The only blood in the apartment was on the bed and beneath the decedent's head. The wound to the head was superficial with no injuries to the brain. Therefore, he did not die of blunt trauma to the head which can occur when a person collapses and falls.

The position of the body is important because it shows that the man collapsed suddenly. If he had been feeling ill he would have positioned himself more comfortably and his body would not have been contorted. The blood beneath his head indicates he did not move once he hit the floor.

Upon further investigation, the blood in the bed proved to agree with the woman's story. A sample could always be tested for the woman's blood type if her story remained in doubt. The woman did run out of the apartment. Although this action might be considered suspect, people do become frightened upon discovering a corpse.

The decedent's blood alcohol was 0.12 grams %. This amount is not high enough to cause death from an acute overdose. Chronic alcoholics are known to die suddenly with little or no alcohol in their system and few signs of chronic disease except for an enlarged fatty liver. No signs of cirrhosis or fatty liver were present at autopsy and no history of chronic drinking was uncovered during the investigation.

This man's death was secondary to his underlying heart disease. His heart was enlarged to 510 grams which is a significant degree of cardiomegaly. There was minimal coronary disease indicating the enlargement was not due to arteriosclerotic disease. Microscopic examination showed scattered interstitial fibrosis without inflammation. Thus the cause of death is idiopathic cardiomyopathy. Individuals with this disease are prone to sudden death by complicating arrhythmias.

Case 2

Decomposed bodies present a medical examiner with some of the most difficult cases. In this case a drug screen was very helpful. It revealed a trace amount of Dilantin indicating that the woman had a seizure disorder. Once this was discovered, the investigator could ask specific questions about the decedent's medical history. Since the remainder of the autopsy and scene investigation were negative, the pathologist would sign the cause of death as an idiopathic seizure disorder. If there was no history of the origin of her seizures, whether as a complication of head trauma or by a natural disorder, the manner of death should be ruled undetermined.

If the drug screen had been negative, the cause of death would be ruled either arteriosclerotic cardiovascular disease or undetermined natural causes. The pathologist would be comfortable with this ruling because the organs were intact and could be evaluated adequately. If he thought the woman died of exposure to a hot or cold environment then the death would be ruled accidental. If the body had decomposed to a skeletonized state, which would preclude adequate examination, and there were no obvious signs of trauma, both the cause and manner of death would be ruled undetermined.

4. *Firearms*
Case

A 25-year old man was found dead in the hallway outside of his apartment. His body was discovered shortly after three shots were heard. A man, observed running from the scene, was arrested soon afterwards and accused of the murder. The defendant stated that the victim threatened to shoot him because he would not pay a drug debt. They fought over the gun, which accidentally fired, striking the deceased. The defendant stated that he took the gun away from the victim and fired two more times because the man was still coming toward him.

A scene investigation revealed three empty cartridges near the body and a few drops of blood on a wall. When the body was moved, a bullet was found beneath the decedent who was

157

wearing blue jeans, shoes, and no shirt. During the scene investigation a neighbor stated that he heard three shots with a pause separating the first from the last two.

An autopsy revealed three gunshot wounds. There was an entrance wound of the abdomen with a 6-inch area of stippling and soot. This bullet passed through the stomach and thoracic vertebral column perforating the spinal cord before exiting the back. A corresponding exit wound was a circular defect with no rim of abrasion. A second gunshot wound entered the right shoulder. There were particles of stippling without fouling around the 3/8 inch in diameter circular defect. Its exit wound was similar to the first except for a small tear on the lateral edge of the defect. A third gunshot wound entered the xyphoid area. There was gunpowder in the wound, but not on the surrounding skin. This bullet passed through the heart before exiting the back near the midline. This exit wound had an irregularly-shaped, circumscribed rim of abrasion measuring 3/16 inch and accentuated up to 3/8 inch on one side.

The prosecutor wanted to know if the wounds were consistent with the defendant's story. Even though there was a witness who heard the shots, the prosecutor doubted the assailant's account. He had no way of disproving the story and needed the pathologist's assistance. Will the pathologist be able to prove whether or not the defendant was telling the truth?

Case Discussion
Case

In this case, the defendant stated the decedent came after him, brandishing a gun. There was an alleged struggle and a gun shot which hit the decedent. The defendant stated that he then took the gun away from the decedent whom he shot two more times because he continued to come after him. A neighbor corroborated the story by saying that he heard a shot, followed by a pause, and two more shots.

If the decedent had been shot during the struggle, there would be signs that the gun was fired close to the body. This can easily be determined by the presence or absence of gunpowder residue around the wound. Since there was no shirt, the residue should have been readily apparent on the skin.

An autopsy revealed three gunshot wounds containing gunpowder either around or in the depths of the wounds. At first, the defendant's story might appear correct because all of the wounds were either of close or contact range. Closer study of the wounds and the statement, however, revealed inconsistencies. There was a 6 inch area of stippling and fouling on the skin around the entrance gunshot wound to the abdomen. This bullet passed through the stomach and thoracic vertebral column and perforated the spinal cord before exiting the body. This wound is consistent with a close range shot as indicated in the defendant's statement. The shot, however, should have paralyzed the victim because it would have perforated his spinal cord. Thus, it could not have been the first shot as stated by the defendant.

The gunshot wound to the right shoulder passed through the shoulder. There was stippling around the wound but no fouling. This is indicative of a muzzle-to-target distance of approximately 6 inches, and would not have caused incapacitation. This wound is consistent with the defendant's story.

The last gunshot wound was a contact gunshot wound in the xyphoid region. The bullet passed through the heart before exiting the body. The bullet found under the decedent's back caused this wound because the exit wound was a "shored" type. A shored exit wound occurs when skin at the exit site is supported by a tight fitting garment or a firm surface such as the floor. In this circumstance, the exit wound would have had an abraded margin. Therefore, the victim was on the floor when this shot was fired.

The analysis of the three gunshot wounds proved the defendant was lying. The gunshot wound to the chest had to have occurred after the victim was lying on the floor and therefore, was the third shot. The shot to the abdomen caused the victim to be paralyzed because the spinal cord had been damaged. He would have fallen to the ground after he was shot. This shot had to have been the second one. The first shot was to the shoulder, followed by a pause, and two more shots. The witness's account was accurate but the way it happened was different from the defendant's description. He stated that he fired two more times when the victim continued to come toward him. If that were true there should not have been a contact gunshot wound to the xyphoid region and a shored exit wound.

A thorough scene investigation is extremely important. What did the blood spatters on the wall look like? In what position was the decedent found? Were there any bullets in the wall? These questions and others need to be answered. Two more bullets should have been recovered. Their locations would have indicated the position of the decedent at the time he was shot.

Another test that might be performed on the deceased is a gunpowder residue test. In theory this test is used to determine whether or not a person had handled or been close to a discharged weapon. In this particular case, if the decedent had not fired the weapon and there was no gunpowder residue on his hands, then his hands were probably not close to or in contact with the weapon when it was fired. This negative finding might support the notion that he was shot twice, paralyzed after the second shot, and then shot while he was in a defenseless position.

An autopsy will determine the number, distance, and path of gunshot wounds. An autopsy, however, is only one part of the death investigation. A proper scene evaluation is an absolute necessity for complete case analysis. In all cases, the scene and autopsy findings must support each other before a final ruling as to cause and manner of death can be made.

5. *Cutting and Stabbing*
Case 1

The body of a 60-year old woman was discovered with a large gaping neck wound. A significant amount of blood was found on her night clothes and on the bathroom floor, particularly beneath her head. Except for the neck wound and a bloody kitchen knife next to her body, there were no other suspicious signs of foul play. Her husband found her shortly after arriving home from work. He called an ambulance immediately although he sensed that she was dead. The ambulance crew arrived, confirmed the woman's death, and noted that her body was cold and rigor mortis had set in. The death was investigated as a homicide. The police thought the husband's affect was inappropriate since he seemed to be very calm about his wife's death. The husband maintained that his wife had not discussed suicide, but had been more despondent about her chronic arthritic pain. Although she had not been completely debilitated she stopped working as a volunteer in the hospital nursery. The police needed to know the extent of her injuries and whether or not the medical examiner thought her injuries could have been self inflicted.

An autopsy revealed a deeply incised neck wound which transected all major vessels and larynx, and extended to the vertebral column. An x-ray of the neck revealed an air bubble within the trachea. Above and below the main defect were a few superficial cuts of the skin which extended either partly or completely across her neck. After his examination, the pathologist ruled the death a suicide. The husband and the police, however, did not agree with the pathologist, especially in light of the extensive neck wound. Was the pathologist's ruling correct?

Case 2

A prison guard was in charge of a 30-cell wing. A riot started in a common room and he was last seen attempting to calm the inmates. A half hour later he was discovered lying on the floor of a cell and was rushed to the prison hospital but was dead on arrival. An attempt at resuscitation was stopped within a few minutes. The prison physician observed two stab wounds to the chest. The inmates were subsequently segregated and the entire wing was searched for weapons. Over thirty sharpened weapons were discovered.

An autopsy performed the next day revealed an inch long defect on the skin of the forehead with ragged edges and an abrasion along the superior margin. This wound extended through the scalp and had a few fine strands of tissue joining the two sides of the defect. One stab wound with blunt angles was located medial to the left nipple and through the chest wall, in a straight path, into the heart for a distance of approximately 3 inches. A second, 1 inch stab wound, with slightly blunted angles, was located on the right side of the chest, 3-4 inches inferior to the nipple. This wound track extended into the upper and lower lobes of the right lung. Approximately 500 ml of unclotted blood was found in the pericardial sac. Other significant findings included severe emphysema and moderate atherosclerotic coronary artery disease.

The authorities wanted to know which stab wound came first, how long the man lived after he was stabbed, and which of the 30 recovered weapons inflicted the injuries.

Case Discussions
Case 1

The medical examiner was convinced that the woman's death was a suicide based on both the scene and history. There was nothing suspicious about the scene of death. The house was too neat to suspect a struggle or foul play. The time of death estimate coincided with observations at the scene. Rigor mortis was in its early stages when the ambulance crew arrived, and the husband's story about being at work for the day was easily confirmed. Finally, the decedent's history of being depressed because of her arthritis was a credible reason for suicide.

The police and husband did not believe the woman could have inflicted such damage to her neck. The pathologist was not surprised seeing such an extensive injury because it is common for suicidal wounds to the neck to be quite severe. Suicidal individuals can inflict extensive damage to themselves. The superficial cuts above and below the main wound are characteristic hesitation marks and consistent with suicide.

The neck x-ray revealed an air bubble within the trachea. This occurs when blood mixes with air. The amount of air can be considerable and, in some cases, a decedent will asphyxiate rather than exsanguinate, especially if only small arteries or veins are incised.

Case 2

The authorities wanted to know how long the guard survived after he was stabbed, but the pathologist was unable to narrow the interval. The guard was "down" for approximately one half hour before being transported to the prison hospital where he was pronounced dead on arrival. The first person to arrive at his side had the best opportunity to check for a pulse and determine if he was breathing.

Since the guard was found dead with no history of when he was last seen, the pathologist would have to estimate the survival time. If there was no blood at the scene then the amount of blood found in the chest cavity would be used. The degree of the man's heart and lung disease would also be taken into account. The pathologist would probably conclude that the man lived for only a few minutes because there was not much blood in the chest cavity and pericardial sac.

The question about which of the thirty weapons caused the injuries is much more difficult. Any of the weapons with two slightly blunt edges may have caused the injuries if their blade widths were less than one inch. Obviously, a weapon which had one blunt angle and one sharp angle could not have caused the injuries and could easily be eliminated. This type of weapon is rarely seen in prison since both sides are usually sharpened. Unlike ballistics, in which an expert can match a bullet to a particular gun, matching a knife to a stab wound is usually impossible.

6. *Drugs and Alcohol*
Case 1

The body of a 20-year old college student was discovered at 3:00 a.m. off the side of a county road. He was last seen at 12:30 a.m. leaving a restaurant where he worked as a waiter. He usually rode his bicycle home from work, but it was not at the scene. It was later found one half mile up the road with a bent back wheel. An autopsy revealed blunt trauma to the body from being dragged, and death secondary to hypovolemia and shock.

At 7:00 a.m. an anonymous caller to the police stated that he saw a hit and run accident involving a truck and a cyclist approximately six hours earlier. The caller gave a good description of the vehicle. The truck was located within an hour, and the driver was taken into custody. Since the driver smelled of alcohol, the police had blood drawn at 8:00 a.m. for an alcohol determination. The results revealed a blood alcohol concentration of 0.09 grams percent (90 mg %). The prosecutor thought the accused was legally intoxicated at the time of the accident but consulted a pathologist. The pathologist agreed the man had been legally drunk during the accident because seven hours before he was tested he would have had an alcohol content of at least 0.2 grams %. The man was indicted for second degree murder. Was the prosecutor correct in his assumption of the man's level of intoxication at the time of the accident? How valid is retrograde extrapolation of a blood alcohol concentration?

Case 2

A known cocaine addict was with a group of people at a party and was last seen going into the bathroom. When she did not come out after an hour, her friend went in to check on her. They found her unresponsive with a syringe sticking in her left arm. At autopsy, a pathologist discovered a fresh needle puncture in her left arm and pulmonary edema, both findings consistent with death from an acute adverse reaction to drugs. Furthermore, a drug screen revealed trace cocaine in the blood with a blood benzoylecgonine concentration of 2.3 mg/L. Although he agreed with the cause of death as a cocaine overdose, the pathologist was not convinced that the eyewitness accounts were correct. The witnesses implied that the decedent had injected herself with drugs while in the bathroom, but the pathologist did not agree with this scenario. Since there was minimal cocaine in the bloodstream, and most was the metabolite, he thought she injected herself before entering the bathroom.

Were the witnesses covering up a more serious crime? Was the pathologist right on track?

Case Discussions
Case 1

Although not involved with determining cause of death, this case illustrates a situation frequently encountered by forensic pathologists: interpreting a drug level found in any person connected with the case, including the defendant. Since a pathologist is often regarded in court as an expert in the effects of drugs on the body, a defense attorney is free to ask anything about drugs. Questions about alcohol's effect on behavior or its metabolism are frequently encountered.

Most pathologists are familiar with the effects of alcohol and the basics of its absorption and metabolism. They know that alcohol is metabolized at approximately one ounce per hour and, when given a number, some tend to extrapolate back to determine the concentration at any previous given time. This simple approach (retrograde extrapolation) is used too often and is fraught with the potential for error. In this case, both the prosecutor and pathologist assumed, without sufficient information, that the defendant had to have had a certain blood alcohol content simply by measuring backwards to the time of the accident. This approach may have been somewhat reasonable if the defendant had been confined and observed for seven hours between accident and arrest. Since he was not observed after the accident, he could have either continued to drink or he may not have had anything to drink until after the accident. More information from witnesses must be obtained

167

before rendering an opinion about his blood alcohol content at the time of the accident.

Case 2

The rate of cocaine metabolism varies between individuals. It may be metabolized very quickly and, at times, may be present in only trace amounts after a person dies by an acute intravenous overdose. In this case, a high concentration of the metabolite is substantial evidence that the woman died shortly after the injection. She allegedly was not discovered for one hour during which time she may have been comatose and continued to metabolize the drug. She may not have injected herself but the pathologist was wrong to assume that everyone was lying because not much of the parent compound was present.

Both the scene and witnessed accounts are consistent with a drug overdose. The pathologist may have relied too heavily on published toxic concentrations and probably did not understand how cocaine is metabolized. Cocaine can degrade quickly in specimen containers without the proper preservative or if improperly stored.

7. *Asphyxia*
Case 1

A young girl came home after school one day and found her mother dead in the laundry room. The woman's body was discovered wedged between the wall and washing machine. She was upside down with her head and torso behind the machine and her legs up in the air.

An autopsy revealed a moderately overweight woman with no external signs of trauma. There was a depressed pale mark across her chest from lying against the washing machine. There were bilateral petechiae of the conjunctivae, face, and scalp, and marked congestion of the lungs. How did the lady die?

Case 2

The body of a dancer was discovered Monday morning in her apartment by the superintendent two days after she was last seen swimming in the apartment pool. She was lying naked supine in bed with the bedspread neatly pulled up to her neck. There were no obvious external signs of trauma. The apartment was in order except for some dirt on the floor next to one of the plants near the sliding door which lead from outside to the bedroom.

The pathologist saw a few petechiae in the right eye, a very slight reddish-blue contusion on the left side of the neck, and slight green discoloration to the abdominal skin. A subsequent police investigation revealed two witnesses who had heard a scream emanating from the swimming pool area at 1:00 a.m. two days earlier. The pathologist decided that the autopsy was inconclusive and ruled the death undetermined both in cause and manner. Was he justified in making this ruling?

Case 3

An elderly gentleman had just finished playing a game in a swimming pool with his grandson. He stood up, grabbed his chest, and went under water without a struggle. The boy called for help. Two relatives nearby had seen the incident and quickly jumped into the water and pulled the man out of the water within a minute. They began cardiopulmonary resuscitation and continued until the paramedics arrived within a few minutes. CPR was discontinued because it was obvious that the gentleman was dead.

An autopsy performed the next morning revealed severe atherosclerotic disease of the coronaries and slight emphysema. There was water in the stomach and no injuries. The medical examiner signed the cause of death as an accidental drowning. Was he justified in doing so?

Case Discussions
Case 1

This lady died of postural asphyxia because she lost her balance, fell, and became caught bending over the back of the washing machine in a position that prevented her from breathing. There were petechiae in her eyes, face and scalp due to increased pressure. The manner of death was accidental.

Case 2

In this case the pathologist felt there was not enough information to render a definitive cause or manner of death. Some of the circumstances, however, should have made the medical examiner suspect a homicide. One of the obvious clues was the position of the bedspread which neatly covered her naked body up to her chin. This was certainly suspicious since the victim would not do this nor asphyxiate herself without leaving an object around used to complete a suicidal act. There was dirt on the floor from a plant that was obviously knocked over and then uprighted. The autopsy revealed only petechiae and a bruise on the neck. These are not naturally occurring phenomena and must have been caused by a second party. There was also a scream which coincided with an approximate time of death.

The pathologist was uncomfortable ruling asphyxiation as the cause of death based on so few findings, but sometimes this may be all the evidence. It is possible, although unlikely, the woman killed herself with a ligature and a loved one found her, removed the evidence, and covered her with the bedspread. This might have happened, but such a scenario would not explain the scream and dirt on the floor. Thus, the correct cause of death is asphyxia due to manual strangulation and the manner is homicide.

Case 3

This man's death should not have been ruled an accident. All witnesses, including the grandson and two relatives, saw the man grab his chest, fall into the water, and sink without a struggle. Severe heart disease was discovered at autopsy. It would be safe to assume that the man had chest pain, followed by a fatal arrhythmia. He was essentially dead by the time he went under water because there was no evidence of any struggle or call for help. His death should have been ruled natural due to heart disease.

171

8. *Electrical And Thermal Injury And Exposure To Extreme Temperatures*

Case 1

A part-time electrician was discovered dead in the crawl space of an old house he was helping to renovate. He was lying face down on dirt clutching a pair of pliers in his left hand against his chest. Numerous wires hung down from the flooring above him. The pliers had burned the man's T-shirt and skin on his chest. Examination of the wires revealed some to be 220 volts and uninsulated.

An autopsy revealed no internal injuries. The chest wound was roughly shaped like the head of the pliers. A second wound, approximately 1/8 inch in diameter, white and umbilicated, was noticed on the thumb of his right hand. What was the cause of this the man's death?

Case 2

The fire department was called to a house fire. After putting out the blaze, they discovered a body in the basement. The remains were charred beyond recognition and sent to a pathologist for analysis.

An examination revealed multiple fractures as well as abundant soot within the airways. There was a skull fracture, however, with an associated epidural hemorrhage. A drug screen revealed only 20% carbon monoxide and the pathologist attributed this level to the decedent's inability to breathe adequately because of head trauma. Other findings at autopsy included: moderate emphysema, gallstones, and coronary artery disease with an associated old myocardial infarction of the left

172

wall.

Since the man died during a fire with a blow to the head, the pathologist ruled the manner of death a homicide. Was this an accurate diagnosis?

Case 3

A 56-year old man entered an apartment of an 80-year old man unannounced. The 56-year old man acted as if he were drunk and the other man threatened him with a baseball bat if he did not leave. Since he chose not to, the elderly gentleman hit him on the back of his head with the bat. The 56-year old man dropped to the floor and did not move. The police and ambulance arrived. The assailant admitted that he struck the dead man on the back of his head with the bat. He was taken to the police station and charged with murder.

An autopsy was performed within an hour of the body's arrival to the morgue. There were only two significant findings: lack of injuries to the head and a high body temperature. The blow to the head barely broke the skin and did not cause injury to the skull or brain. The pathologist noted that the internal organs seemed hot. Organ temperatures were performed and the liver, for instance, was 108° Fahrenheit.

The pathologist felt the man died of hyperthermia and subsequent investigation revealed the decedent had been taking Thorazine™ for his schizophrenia. The prosecutor and police wanted to know why this was not a homicide and what caused the hyperthermia.

Case 4

On a cold January morning a policeman discovered a man lying on a park bench. The man was not moving and the policeman thought he was dead due to exposure to the cold. He called the morgue but the technician who arrived thought he saw the man move and called an ambulance. The paramedics felt the man was alive and transported him to a nearby hospital. In the emergency room the patient's rectal temperature was 82° Fahrenheit. The patient died despite efforts to rewarm him.

An autopsy revealed a cachectic man with cirrhosis. A drug screen was positive for alcohol and a trace amount of benzoylecgonine. The pathologist wanted to sign out the manner and cause of death as natural due to acute and chronic alcoholism. His associate, however, disagreed and stated that the manner and cause should be different. What was the appropriate cause and how should the manner have been ruled?

Case Discussions
Case 1

The man in this case was electrocuted. He had grabbed an uninsulated wire with his bare hand. His body was grounded causing the charge to enter his thumb, travel down his arm, and exit his chest. The uninsulated pliers attracted the charge and, by being in contact with his chest, were burned into his chest wall. Two hundred-twenty volts were more than enough to cause death since the resistance and voltage created the necessary amperage and caused a cardiac arrhythmia.

Case 2

The pathologist made an error in this case. The low carbon monoxide value was due to the decedent's underlying emphysema and coronary artery disease. Individuals with an underlying chronic disease commonly die before they breathe in much CO. The soot within the airways also proved the victim was alive at the time of the fire.

The skull fracture was secondary to heat not trauma. An epidural hemorrhage is a common consequence of heat and must not be misinterpreted as a sign of trauma.

A pathologist should wait until all tests of an investigation are completed prior to making a final ruling. If a fire marshall determines that a fire is an arson, then any death would be a homicide regardless of anatomic findings.

Case 3

This case is unusual because the death caused by malignant hyperthermia was at first confused with a homicide. The blow to the head barely lacerated the skin with no brain damage. The history of Thorazine™ use was important since it is associated with malignant hyperthermia.

In this case the diagnosis was easily made because of the lack of head trauma and high liver temperature. Often, an examiner is not so fortunate. A body may lie for hours before it is discovered and the temperature may recede. The only indication of hyperthermia may be an accelerated rate of decomposition out of proportion to the postmortem interval (if it is known).

Case 4

The physician at the hospital provided the most important information for determining the cause of death because he took a rectal temperature. If he had not found the man to have a temperature of 82° (normally 98°), the correct diagnosis of hypothermia would most likely have been missed because the body would have been sent to the morgue and refrigerated prior to the autopsy.

The history was the most important factor which the pathologist overlooked. The decedent had positive blood alcohol and benzoylecgonine levels. Without a scene investigation his death would have been ruled natural, and attributed to the chronic effects of drug abuse, as the original pathologist suggested. These drugs, however, only contributed to the main cause of death, i.e., the low environmental temperatures and subsequent hypothermia. Therefore, his manner of death was correctly ruled an accident.

9. *Blunt Trauma*
General And Motor Vehicle–Pedestrian
Case 1

An elderly woman was discovered lying on her back in her sewing room. Rigor mortis was in its early stages. A prominent amount of blood was covering her face. At autopsy there were red-blue contusions to her chest and right side with associated lacerations of the spleen and liver. After washing her face, a patterned contusion of the left cheek was noted resembling a heel mark from a shoe or boot. There was no significant head trauma. Numerous photographs of the facial

176

contusion were taken.

Within hours of the autopsy, a suspect was apprehended. He was present in the neighborhood the last day the woman was seen alive. He was wearing boots which the authorities confiscated for testing. Fingerprint powder was dusted on the sole, a transparency print was made, and the transparency was placed over the photograph of the facial wound. A criminalist determined the comparison was a positive match and the pathologist agreed. On the basis of these examinations the suspect was indicted. No other incriminating evidence was found against him. Should these interpretations have been made?

Case 2

A 20-year old woman was discovered lying on the sidewalk next to a busy traffic intersection. There were compound fractures of her right femur and tibia. At postmortem examination the pathologist noted multiple rib fractures, predominantly on the right side, and lacerations of both liver and spleen. Two liters of blood were found in the peritoneal cavity. There were a few contusions of the left lung and a laceration of the posterior scalp. There was minimal subarachnoid hemorrhage over the convexity of the brain, but there were no significant injuries. The pathologist ruled the death an accident by motor vehicle. The cause of death was listed as blunt injuries to the torso and an extremity fracture.

A witness saw a white pickup truck near the intersection about the time the body had been discovered, and after a few days of searching, the driver and vehicle were located. During questioning by the police, the driver admitted hitting the woman. He stated that the woman stepped off the curb in front of him before seeing her and was unable to stop. He became scared and left the scene after he checked the woman and noticed that she was not breathing. The police and prosecutor wanted to know if the defendant's story could be substantiated by the autopsy findings.

Case Discussions
Case 1

The approach by both the pathologist and criminalist were sound. Both looked at the boot, transparency, and photograph of the wound to make to comparison. A mark on the face can be matched with an offending weapon if the pattern is distinct. In this case, both examiners thought the match was perfect because the marks on the face corresponded to the depressed areas of the heel of a shoe.

Matching patterns on a body with objects that may have inflicted them is an important part of examining injuries caused by blunt trauma. These patterns, however, cannot be used to determine whether a specific weapon inflicted injury. At best one can determine that a weapon of similar dimension caused damage. Although patterned injuries on the body are not commonly matched to a particular weapon, there may be other material transferred from a victim to a weapon such as hair, fibers, and blood. Thus, the examination suggested that the mark was made by a boot with a certain type of sole.

Case 2

The pathologist told the prosecutor that the suspect was lying. The woman's injuries were basically confined to the right side of her body as indicated by fractures of the right femur and ribs. If she had stepped to the curb in front of the truck she would have been struck on her left side. She most likely crossed the street on the driver's left side, and was struck in his lane on her right side.

The pathologist should also have measured the distance from the fractured femur to the end of the foot. This distance, coupled with an examination of the clothing, is helpful in determining if the brakes were applied at the time of the accident, causing the bumper fracture to be lower than the actual height of the bumper. The point of impact on the truck matched to the site of the body indicates whether the driver attempted to stop.

10. *Blunt Head Trauma*
Case 1

A 42-year old homeless man was discovered in the middle of a road beneath a bridge. There was blood exuding from his left ear and left temporal scalp lacerations. An autopsy revealed that blood from the left ear was due to a fracture of the left middle fossae at the base of the skull. Besides diffuse cerebral edema, the brain was contused over the lateral and inferior aspects of the left temporal lobe. There were also contusions of the brain directly beneath a fracture of the right occipital bone. There was a posterior scalp laceration on the right side which extended to the bone. The remainder of the autopsy revealed fractures of left ribs 3-7 and the left scapula. Moderate soft tissue hemorrhages were associated with the fractures, as well as a laceration and multiple contusions of the left lung. Fifty ml of blood remained in the left chest cavity.

The police attributed the man's death to a fall off the bridge. After an autopsy, the medical examiner ruled the death a homicide from blunt impacts to the head. Why did the examiner make this ruling despite what the police thought, and what part did the other injuries play in this man's death?

Case 2

A husband and wife were seen arguing in their driveway near the back of their car. The next door neighbor, who witnessed the argument, said the couple began shouting at each other. The man became quite upset and slapped his wife across her left cheek. The witness said the slap did not appear to be particularly severe, but the woman slumped behind the car within a few seconds and never moved again. The husband bent down and began yelling that his wife was not breathing. The neighbor ran over to the woman and noted that she stopped breathing so she began cardiopulmonary resuscitation and told the man to call 911. The paramedics arrived within ten minutes and continued resuscitation while they transported her to the nearest emergency room. The woman was pronounced dead shortly after her arrival.

An autopsy revealed a massive subarachnoid hemorrhage of the brain which the medical examiner ruled as the cause of death. A ruptured aneurysm was not identified. The husband was tried for manslaughter and was convicted. How could a slap to the cheek cause this woman's death?

Case Discussions
Case 1

This case was signed out as a homicide due to a blow to the head. The examiner correctly concluded that the multiple thoracic injuries could have occurred from a fall. The head injury, however, did not fit the pattern of a fall. The man had an occipital bone fracture at the base of the skull and an associated underlying brain contusion. If this impact was from a fall, a contrecoup injury should have been present in the front of the brain. Furthermore, there was an impact site on the left side of the head with an associated coup brain contusion. If these injuries had occurred from a fall there would have been a contrecoup contusion on the opposite side of the brain. Thus the pathologist reasoned that the man was in a stationary position relative to the moving object which struck him. That is, someone hit him in the head. The rib fractures could also be the result of a beating.

Case 2

This woman died from a blow to the head which caused a tear in the vertebral artery which traverses the upper cervical vertebrae before entering the skull. The exact location of the bleeding site can be difficult to locate because the tear may be very small. It is essential to examine the brain very carefully and remove all adherent blood clots while the brain is fresh in order to identify the defect. Once the brain is preserved in formaldehyde, examination of the vessels is less than adequate.

A posterior neck dissection is needed to examine the vertebral arteries as they course through the vertebrae.

The manner of death is considered homicide because there has been a death of one person due to the action of another. The degree of homicide, based on the circumstances of death, will be determined by the prosecuting attorneys. Convicting an assailant based on the history of a single blow can be difficult even though a witness may give an accurate account of the circumstances.

11. *Pediatric Forensic Pathology*
Case 1

A 3-year old girl was brought into the emergency room and was pronounced dead on arrival. The man who accompanied the child was her stepfather. He said the child was standing on a chair at the dinner table, fell backward, and hit her head on the edge of a china cabinet and uncarpeted floor. The stepfather said he became worried and decided to watch her for the next few hours. The child seemed to be doing well until later in the evening when he noticed she had stopped breathing.

Since there was a history of trauma, the medical examiner took jurisdiction of the death and performed an autopsy. The postmortem examination revealed multiple injuries. Externally there were bluish contusions of the neck, forehead, and cheek. The buttocks were covered with yellow contusions. The frenulum of the mouth had been previously torn and there was an associated healing laceration at the upper gum line. The skin of the back was reflected and at least three areas of hemorrhage were present over the upper portion. The brain was markedly swollen and at least 10 ml of blood were noted over the cerebral hemispheres. Skeletal x-rays were negative and an examination of the eyes showed bilateral retinal hemorrhages. Are these injuries consistent with the stepfather's story?

Case 2

The janitor of a university dormitory went into a women's restroom and discovered a baby in the toilet. He immediately called the police and they in turn called the medical examiner. The medical examiner observed a newborn, approximately third trimester, infant with an attached placenta. There was blood within the toilet and on the floor of the stall. Later in the day a young coed living on the fifth floor admitted she gave birth to the baby shortly after midnight. She became scared, stayed in her room, and did not tell anyone what happened.

The police asked the girl what she specifically did to the baby while it was being born. The girl replied that she did not remember the exact sequence of events but she did feel the baby was not alive when it was delivered because the baby was not moving. She assumed the baby was born dead, but did not know for sure.

The pathologist did not see any internal or external injuries, except for some subscapular hemorrhages which he attributed to the birthing process. There was approximately 10 ml of water in the stomach but no water in the lungs. He placed the lungs in both water and formalin and they sank. He concluded the baby had never taken a breath and was stillborn. Was this an accurate diagnosis and examination in this case?

Case Discussions

Case 1

The father's story does not match the child's injuries. There were too many injuries which could not have occurred from the fall described. There should have been two separate impact sites where the child hit the cabinet and then the floor. An autopsy revealed at least three separate impact sites on the neck, forehead, and cheek. These alone are not consistent with the story. In addition, the brain injuries are not the type seen in a fall. If the child had fallen there would have been either a significant subarachnoid, subdural, or epidural hemorrhage and a possible skull fracture. This child had only a slight amount of subdural hemorrhage, a diffusely edematous brain, and retinal hemorrhages. These findings are commonly seen in a shaken child.

The diffuse cerebral edema seen in this case occurs quickly after a child is shaken. The father's statement about watching the child for a few hours before she became symptomatic does coincide with the findings. He probably did bring her to the hospital shortly after she stopped breathing but it was soon after he had stopped shaking her.

This death would automatically be suspicious because of the multiple injuries and would require an immediate investigation. The healing laceration of the gum, torn frenulum, and contusions of the buttocks and back are all suspicious for prior abuse. This child had obviously been battered over many days prior to the fatal episode.

Case 2

The determination of a live birth versus a stillborn is difficult, particularly when a child may have died within a few minutes after birth. The question in this case is whether or not the baby drowned in the toilet or was born dead. X-rays should have been taken to determine if air was present in the lungs in addition to the gastrointestinal tract. If a baby is born alive, there should be some indication of air in the lungs. An obsolete test was performed to determine if the lungs would float in water. If they floated, presumably air had been inhaled. This test has been shown to be meaningless. The gross appearance of the lungs can provide some indication of whether they have been aerated. Areas of aeration will appear pink as opposed to a dark purple-red color of those areas which never expand after birth. The presence or absence of air within the gastrointestinal tract is helpful because babies will swallow air, even if they live a short time, and it will travel into the small bowel. Unfortunately, if cardiopulmonary resuscitation is attempted, air may be forced into both the small bowel and lungs, negating this finding.

The pathologist in this case made assumptions based on unreliable techniques. The baby should have been x-rayed to check for the presence of air. Even if x-rays had been taken, however, the diagnosis of stillbirth may not have been made with certainty. In the absence of evidence of trauma, however, stillbirth is clearly the most reasonable conclusion.

PART VI
Helpful Hints in Testifying

People who work in death investigation become quite proficient in the technical and professional aspects of their job, but receive little or no training in what to expect as a witness in a courtroom or during a deposition. They are often simply told "tell the truth and all will be fine." This is inappropriate, especially since their testimony may lead to conviction or acquittal.

Death investigators should be impartial. This may be easier for independent agencies, especially those not under any other branch of law enforcement or state or city agency. Those who work for law enforcement may feel pressured when testifying for the state. Fortunately this is a rare occurrence. No matter how unbiased pathologists and death investigators want to be, however, their testimony will be looked upon as favorable to either the defense or the prosecution. Consequently, they will be viewed as advocates and should be aware of what to expect in a potential adversarial situation in a courtroom or during a deposition.

Five Points of Preparation

1. Preparation time is necessary. Most witnesses will know days in advance when they will testify. They should use the time wisely for review and not wait until the last moment to prepare. Time is needed to formulate and finalize opinions and talk to the attorney who sent the subpoena (see #3). For some cases, little time is needed for review, especially if a witness is only called upon to relate facts. If, however, as in most cases, a witness is needed to present an opinion, more preparation time

is essential.

Most subpoenas do not result in a person actually testifying since many cases are settled out of court. Many witnesses become lax if a case is continued, especially multiple times. If a case is continued, material should be reviewed each time prior to testifying so that some important points are remembered.

2. <u>Know the material</u>. Knowing and understanding a case is different from regurgitating memorized facts. Investigators in death cases are rarely asked to recite the facts. They are usually asked to give opinions based on the facts.

3. <u>Talk to the attorney before testifying</u>. This does not mean moments before entering a courtroom. The witness may have few things to say, but he would not have been called if his testimony meant little to the case. An attorney should know exactly what a witness is going to say and go over the questions carefully. This is a good time for a witness to let an attorney know exactly how far his opinion could be pushed. Witnesses need to be aware that some attorneys may attempt to push their opinion.

4. <u>Prepare for the unexpected</u>. Witnesses generally know the weak points of their testimony as do good attorneys. A witness should study the weak points and be prepared for a cross-examiner to introduce them. Even if the weak points may potentially hurt a direct examiner's case, they must be answered honestly without hesitation or apology and with an appropriate explanation if needed.

5. <u>Review the high points</u>. The most important facts and opinions should be reviewed again in the last few minutes prior to testifying. A witness should not waste time in the witness

187

room conversing with law enforcement officers or other witnesses. The time should be utilized to solidify specific facts which a witness should know without looking at a report. Juries are more impressed with a witness who can speak naturally without having to read from a report.

A witness should expect an outline of the questions to be asked from an attorney performing a direct examination. Many attorneys prepare a verbatim list of the questions. A witness should review these questions with the attorney so that both can give suggestions about the order or the appropriateness of the questions. Witnesses who are independent should be willing to help attorneys from both sides with the order of questions.

The Hypothetical Question

Attorneys may ask for an opinion after asking a hypothetical question. This question may be quite long and may list facts that are required by a witness to render a specific opinion. Not all attorneys like to use hypothetical questions, but if they do, they review them with a witness prior to testifying and provide a written copy. A witness should help an attorney include necessary facts to render a specific opinion. Hopefully, an attorney will provide a copy of the questions to the witness for review prior to testifying.

One author (JD) has had experience with hypothetical questions that could have been disasters. For example, an attorney had discussed several facts during a phone conversation and we agreed that these facts were necessary to render an opinion. Specifically, a man had died after being hit by a car in a parking lot. The decedent had received multiple crushing injuries. In addition, a description of the man's clothing was as important to the case as the circumstances. During the trial, the direct examiner listed all pertinent injury facts but failed to mention the clothing. The author did not know what to do. Without the clothing, an opinion of death by motor vehicle accident could not be rendered. Fortunately, the opposing counsel objected, stating that some facts, such as the clothing, were excluded. The direct examiner then mentioned the clothing and the author provided his opinion. Since that episode, the author requires attorneys to write out questions prior to a courtroom appearance.

Testifying in the Courtroom
What the witness should do.

1. Be confident. Jurors know when a witness lacks confidence by his hesitant replies and uncomfortable disposition. A juror believes that if a witness is unsure of the evidence then his testimony is looked upon with equal uncertainty. On the other hand, a witness should not be over confident because a juror may view the witness as arrogant.

2. Answer every question truthfully. This seems self-explanatory. A witness holds himself liable for problems created for the case as well as for himself.

3. Be firm in your answers. Do not say 'I believe' or 'I think' very often. A witness should give definitive answers.

4. Know his limitations. Many witnesses have areas of expertise outside their formal education. Without credentials this expertise may be difficult for jurors to evaluate.

5. Do not volunteer information. The more information provided makes a witness more vulnerable to cross-examination. Questions should be answered succinctly, unless more explanation is necessary.

6. Say if more than a yes or no answer is required. Cross-examiners may object if a witness does not provide a yes or no answer as instructed. Some answers cannot be stated in this manner without qualification or explanation. If a witness attempts to go beyond a yes or no answer and a cross-examiner still objects, he should turn to the judge and explain that a yes or no answer is inappropriate. The judge may agree with the witness and allow him to continue, or disagree, at which point the witness must do as instructed.

7. Look at the jury. The witness should look at the jury as much as possible when answering questions. The jury decides the importance of a witness's testimony. If a witness feels uncomfortable scanning the jury then he should focus on one or two jurors.

8. Remain as calm as possible. There is nothing wrong with being nervous. A slight amount of nervousness tends to keep people alert. Excessive nervousness, however, detracts from a testimony. The more often a person testifies, the easier it becomes.

9. Make sure the question is understood. Take time to think of an appropriate response. If the question is not clear and difficult to understand, ask for it to be repeated. Some cross-examiners purposely ask complex or rapid-fire questions to confuse a witness. Taking time to answer the question accurately will both slow the cross-examiner down and give the witness

time to give the best possible intended response.

Many judges become acquainted with frequent witnesses. They may allow more latitude than someone with whom they are unfamiliar. A frequent witness should not become too comfortable. He should pretend that he is unknown to the judge. This is especially helpful if a change of venue occurs and the new judge is unfamiliar with the witness.

Things a witness should not do.

1. Be flippant. Cynicism and sarcasm may not be appreciated by the judge or the jury. The witness should also refrain from trying to be humorous.

2. Help the examiner. If an examiner says something wrong or different from what was discussed then he will suffer the consequences. A witness should not correct the examiner because one way to look biased is to answer an unasked question. A witness may help an examiner or cross-examiner with a wrong definition or an incorrectly pronounced word.

3. Become upset or angry. It is easy to become upset when a cross-examiner accuses you of doing the job poorly, inefficiently, or inappropriately. The direct examiner and judge can protect a witness if the cross-examiner is saying or exhibiting outrageous or inappropriate behavior. A witness should seek the judge's help if he feels he is being treated improperly.

What to Expect under Cross-Examination

The cross-examiner's job is to persuade jurors that the witness's testimony is irrelevant. Any person involved in an investigation may be the most important witness in a case. He should be prepared for rigorous and, at times, confrontational questioning. An expert cross-examiner can usually anticipate a witness's statement. He has prepared by reading prior testimony from either depositions, preliminary or grand jury trials, prior court appearances, or publications. Moreover, he may have consulted other experts.

After reviewing this information, a good cross-examiner plans his strategy. He will be direct and brief and will not resort to courtroom antics. He may ask a witness to repeat several points for the jury's sake.

An attorney who has a weak case or is poorly prepared may resort to any of the following tactics to make a witness's testimony less credible.

1. Attempt to make a witness upset or mad. A witness who becomes upset may be unable to think clearly and may respond inappropriately or contradict previous testimony. If this happens, he should attempt to calm down immediately and rectify any misstatements.

2. Ask questions in rapid succession; cause a witness to give a series of yes or no answers. Rapidly asked questions may force quickly and poorly thought out answers. A witness should try to slow down the questioning and pause long enough to give himself time to think more effectively. Questions requiring yes or no responses may catch a witness off-guard and force him to say yes when he means no, or vice-versa. Again, a

witness needs to slow down the questioner by providing explanations or asking for a question to be repeated.

3. Go over the material repeatedly. A witness may become impatient and possibly upset at this line of questioning.

4. Bring in contradictory statements. A witness should be prepared by reading his prior testimony or reports.

5. Place importance on being a witness for the state. This is common for state or government employees who are usually called to testify for the prosecution. A witness should make no apologies and answer appropriately.

7. Ask about being paid. Usually this line of questioning is reserved for consultants. They are usually asked about their fees and are accustomed to answering questions about how much they are paid, not for their testimony, but for their time.

Remember, a cross-examiner's job is to discredit a witness's testimony. Any approach is fair as long as it is not objected by opposing counsel and meets a judge's approval. A witness should understand that an attorney is not trying to be personal in his attack. Most cross-examiners understand that they may need the witness as a consultant at some future date and will treat them with respect. Moreover, a witness must remain poised and professional and should never stoop to game-playing. Unless a witness is very knowledgeable and comfortable in the courtroom he should not try to play the attorney's game. An attorney tends to have the advantage because he is in his territory, the courtroom. Jurors can tell when attorneys are playing games and when a witness is being picked on and will probably give the witness the benefit of doubt.

Ranges

A witness is often asked by a cross-examiner to give a time frame which is usually impossible to provide. For instance, there are no absolute answers to the following questions: How long was a person dead before the body was discovered? How long did the person live after the injury? How long did the pool of blood take to dry? When absolute answers cannot be given an attorney may ask for a range. Most witnesses become trapped into giving too narrow a range. Remember, an attorney cannot force a witness to answer a particular question unless the judge overrules an objection.

A common example concerns questions about the postmortem interval. An expert qualified to render an opinion about time of death and the postmortem interval will often provide a range of times as an estimation. When one is provided, a cross-examiner will try to dismiss the extreme values, especially if the time frame jeopardizes his case. If a witness believes a range is accurate he should not change it, regardless of what the attorney says.

One author (JD) was pressed to give a range when he thought a person had been dead for a few days, but was not sure of the environmental conditions. The judge instructed the author to give a range despite his uncertainty. The author then said the person had expired within one hour to one year. The cross-examiner was obviously upset with this response. The author restated that he was uncomfortable giving a range and provided this answer under pressure. The judge only required the author to provide a range, no matter how broad. The attorney was forced to stop the line of questioning and proceed to another topic.

Authoritative Texts

A common method of impeaching a witness's testimony is to read a recognized authority's opposing viewpoint. Unanimous agreement on an authority's point of view regarding a particular topic is rare. An attorney will usually preface his point by asking a witness if an author is an expert on the topic and if his work is considered authoritative in his field. If a witness agrees that an author is an expert, he should qualify his answer by saying that he may disagree with some of the author's opinions. An author's viewpoint regarding a subject should be read before a witness renders an opinion.

Depositions

Depositions are fact-finding procedures consisting of attorneys, a court reporter, and a witness. They provide prosecuting and defense attorneys with an opportunity to preview a witness's testimony. Depositions are more common in civil than in criminal cases. A witness is sworn in as if he were in a courtroom. The atmosphere, however, is more relaxed because of the absence of a judge and jury. These surroundings may cause a witness to believe that a deposition is less important than testifying in court. Once a witness has a response read back to him that differs from the one given in court he will wish that he had regarded the deposition more seriously.

A witness should follow the same rules for preparation and review, as if he were going to court, including a discussion with the attorney. Hypothetical questions can be asked and subjected to the same scrutiny by a cross-examiner, who probably will not be as difficult as in court.

A witness will be able to read the transcript, usually within a few weeks of the deposition, and should sign the transcript if asked. A witness should not waive the signature, meaning he declines to review the testimony, since this may be the only opportunity to review his statements and change any inaccuracies.

In a trial, statements made during a deposition may be taken out of context. One should ask that the entire section related to the statement be read if an answer seems incorrect. Occasionally the tone of questioning during a deposition differs from that of a trial. Answers may also be different depending on the context of the line of questioning. Be prepared to explain why an answer may be different. Moreover, if an opinion has changed since the deposition, a witness should be prepared for a hard line of questioning from the cross-examiner.

Appendix A: Photographs

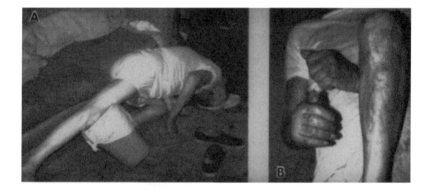

Postmortem Interval. A. Rigor mortis. B. When rolled over, leg remains flexed. If the room temperature is between 70° and 75° F, complete rigor indicates interval since death of at least 12 hours.

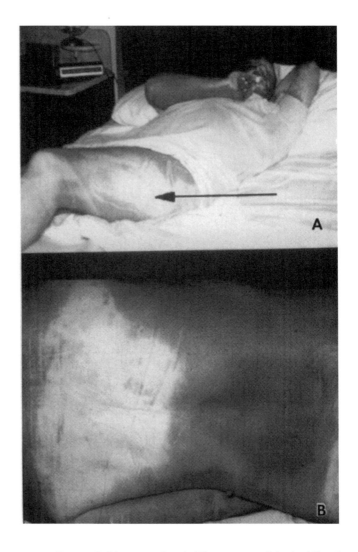

Postmortem Interval. Livor mortis. A. The pattern of the bedding is stained on the man's legs. B. This man has been on his back for at least eight hours for livor mortis to be "fixed."

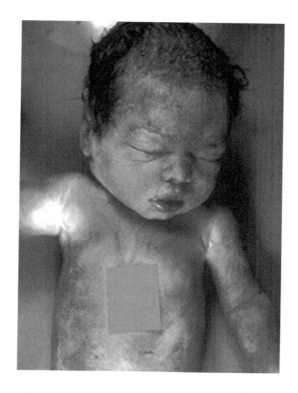

Identification. This baby, whose body was discovered in a toilet, could not have been identified prior to the discovery of DNA finger printing. DNA was helpful in providing this child's identity.

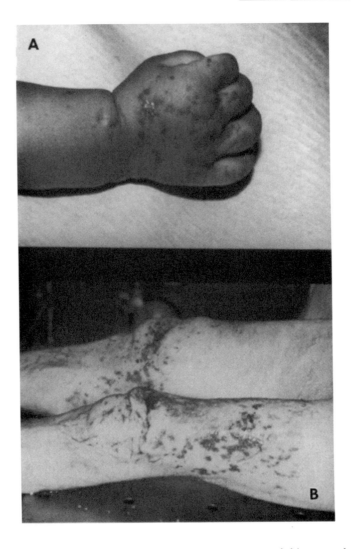

Postmortem Changes. A. Anthropophagia. Ant or roach bites on a baby who died of SIDS. B. Lesions on a man left by the side of a road after being struck in the head and strangled.

200

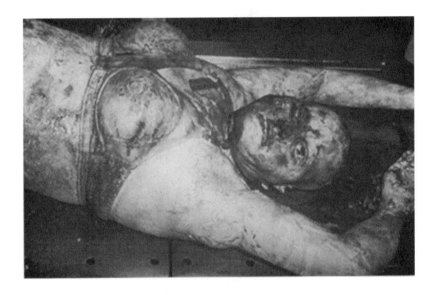

Postmortem Changes. Adipocere. Middle-aged white female whose body was discovered attached to weights in fresh water. She had been submerged in water for 10.5 months. Soft tissues have hardened or saponified. Owing to adipocere change, she can still be identified.

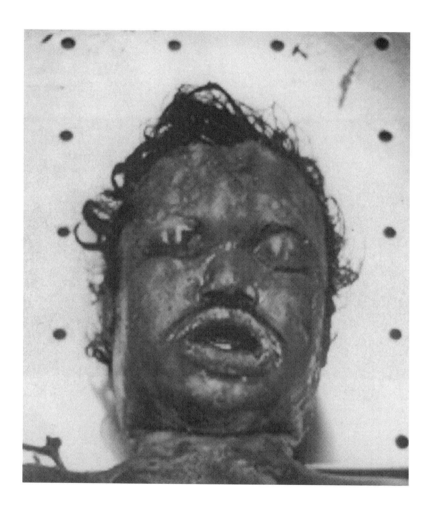

Postmortem Changes. Decomposition. Twenty-one year old thin, white male found in river after 4-5 days. Note change of skin pigment and swelling.

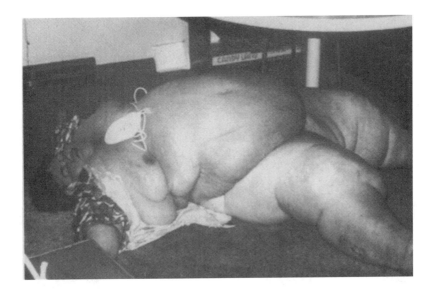

Sudden Natural Death. This obese woman died suddenly. Obesity and an enlarged heart were the only autopsy findings.

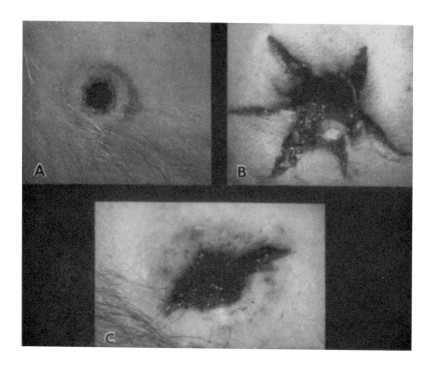

Gunshot Wounds. A. Contact wound from low velocity bullet with muzzle stamp surrounding wound. B. Multiple lacerations caused by pressure buildup from a high velocity, large caliber bullet. C. Contact wound with laceration of skin.

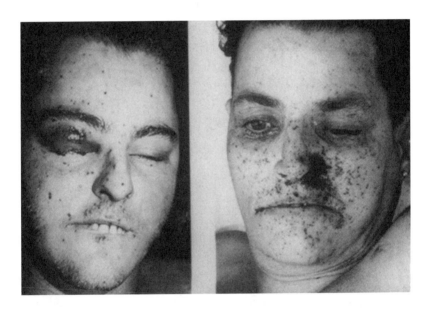

Gunshot Wounds. Intermediate Wounds. Both victims were shot from a distance of less than three feet. There is stippling but no soot on their faces.

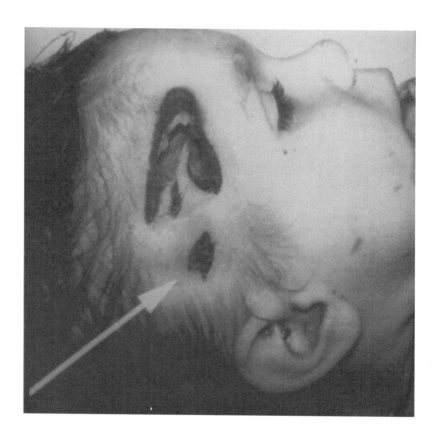

Gunshot Wounds. An irregular gunshot wound to the head. The larger defect is an entrance wound and the smaller one is an exit wound (arrow).

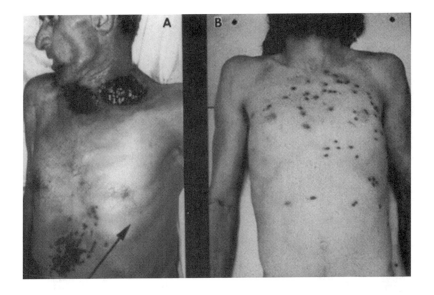

Shotgun Wounds. A. Shot to the abdomen. Direction of pellets up towards left side of the body, as indicated by arrow. B. Marked spreading of pellets. Only two pellets entered the chest cavity and heart.

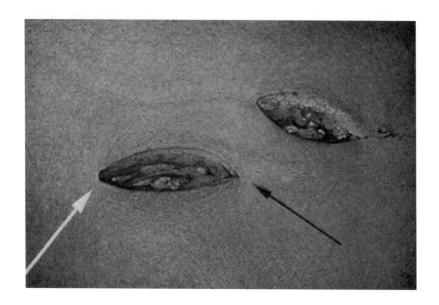

Cutting and Stabbing. Wound angles aid in weapon determination. White arrow points to a blunt angle and black arrow points to a sharp angle, indicative of a weapon with a single sharp cutting edge.

208

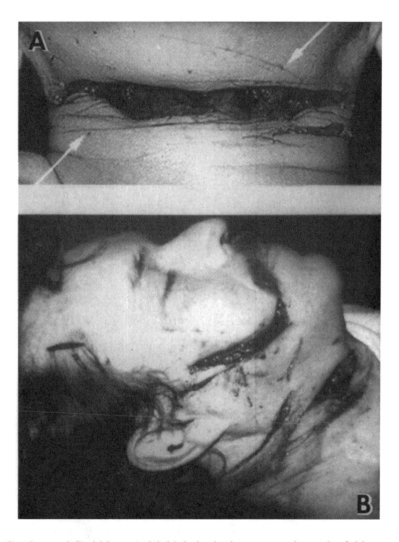

Cutting and Stabbing. A. Multiple hesitation cuts on the neck of this suicide victim. B. Multiple incisions of face and neck, usually indicating a homicide.

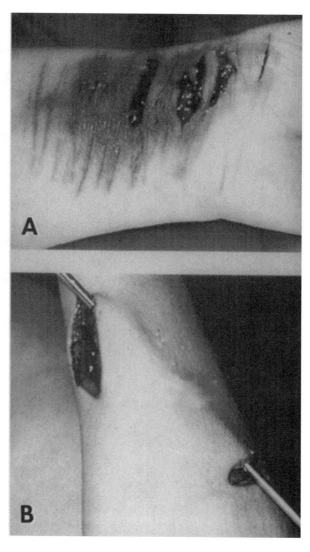

Cutting and Stabbing. A. Multiple deep cuts and hesitation marks. B. Stab wound which occurred when the decedent raised arm defensively.

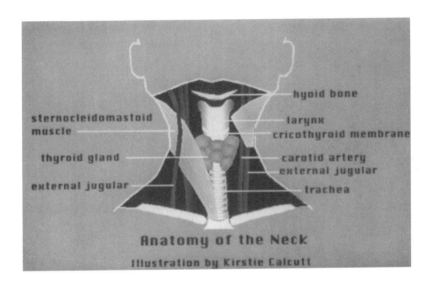

Anatomy of the Neck
Illustration by Kirstie Calcutt

Asphyxia. Neck anatomy. Blood vessels, trachea, and hyoid bone may be damaged or compressed in various asphyxial deaths.

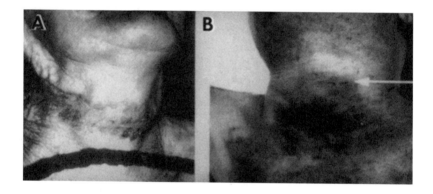

Asphyxia. A. Rope pattern of this hanging victim is clearly visible. B. Contusions and fingernail marks (arrow) in a case of manual strangulation. Fingernail marks were caused by the victim attempting to remove the assailant's hands.

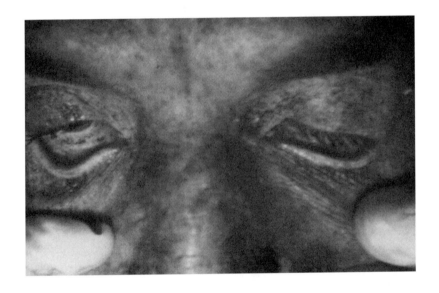

Asphyxia. A strangulation victim with multiple petechiae of eyes and eyelids.

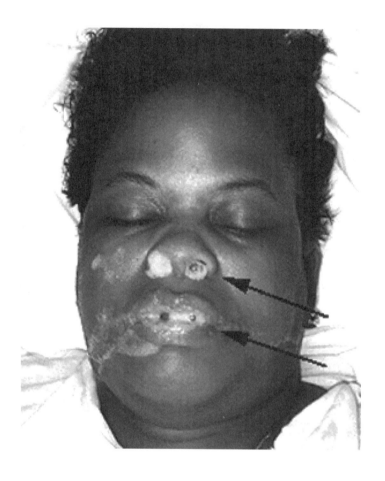

Drowning. Foam (arrows) is commonly seen in drowning victims and cases of drug overdose.

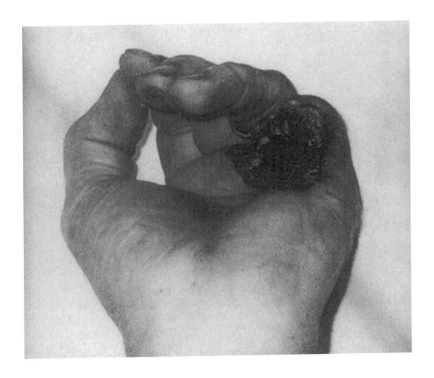

Electrocution. Injuries from electrocution are quite variable. There may be no injuries in low voltage deaths or obvious burning, as shown from contact of this man's hand with a high voltage line.

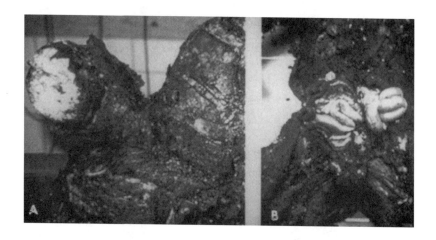

Thermal Injury. Artifacts. A. Skull fracture with exposed brain. B.
Opened abdominal cavity exposing intestines.

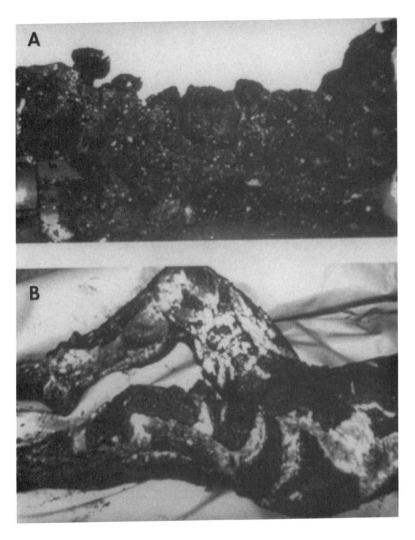

Thermal Injury. A. Although this body is markedly charred, a blood sample may be obtained and soot may be detected. B. Multiple skin splits as an artifact of fire.

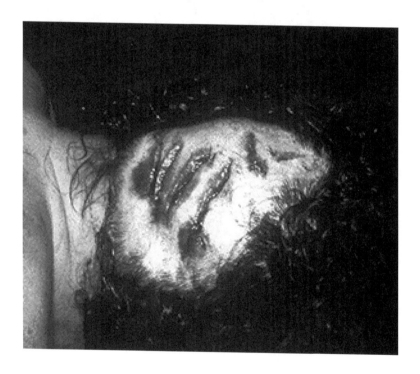

Blunt Trauma. Multiple lacerations with no specific pattern caused by the stock of a rile.

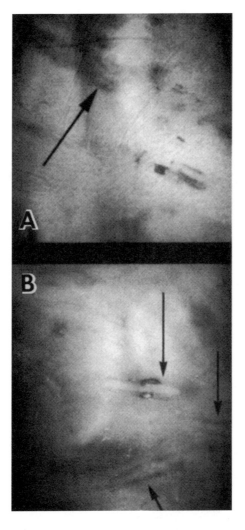

Blunt Trauma. Both photographs show individuals struck by objects which left pale centers and contused edges (arrow). The objects were a rifle barrel (A) and a belt (B).

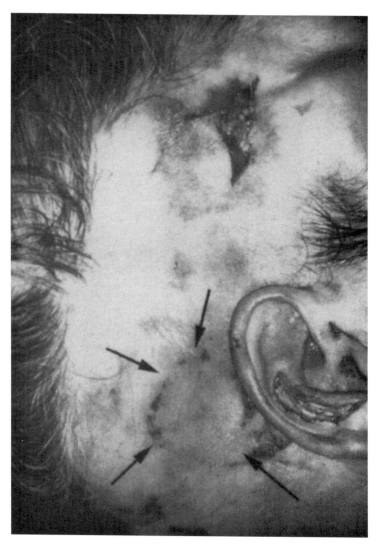

Blunt Trauma. Contusions, abrasions, and lacerations. Arrows outline the pattern of a small sledge hammer which caused the injuries.

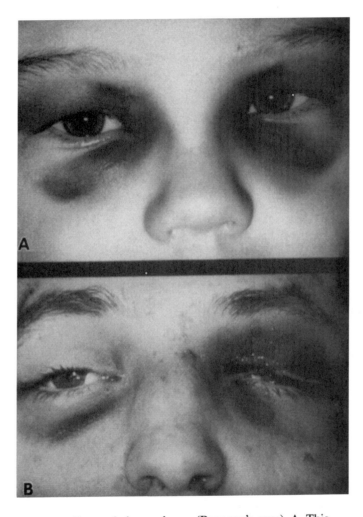

Head Trauma. Spectacle hemorrhages (Raccoon's eyes). A. This child was struck with enough force to cause soft tissue hemorrhage without fracturing the skull. B. This decedent was shot in the head. Orbital skull fractures caused these hemorrhages.

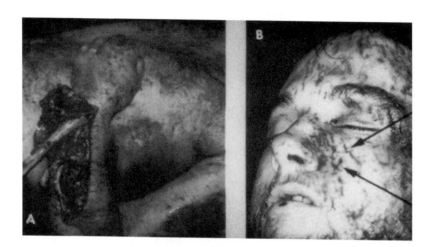

Motor Vehicle. Occupant injuries. A. Fractured forearm.
B. "Dicing" abrasions (arrows) from hitting side window.

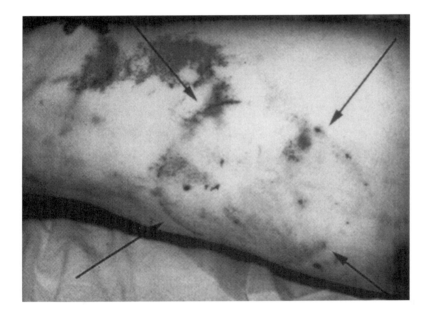

Pedestrian Injuries. Leg with pattern injury from a headlight (arrows).

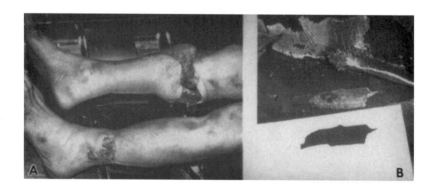

Pedestrian Injuries. A. Bilateral lower leg fractures from a car bumper. Distance from fracture sites to heels should be measured.
B. Automobile part recovered from decedent's clothing.

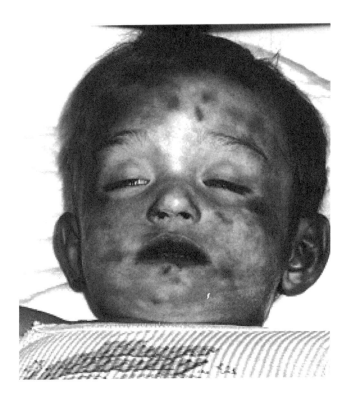

Pediatric Injuries. Physical abuse. These injuries could not have occurred naturally.

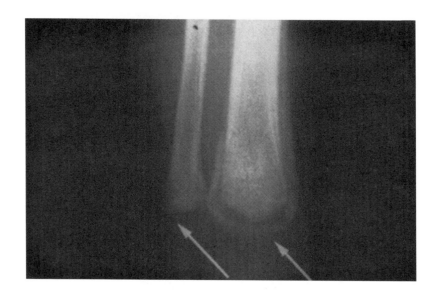

Pediatric Injuries. Abuse. X-ray shows healing (arrows) of small fractures at ends of the tibia and fibula. The child's leg was severely twisted by a caretaker.

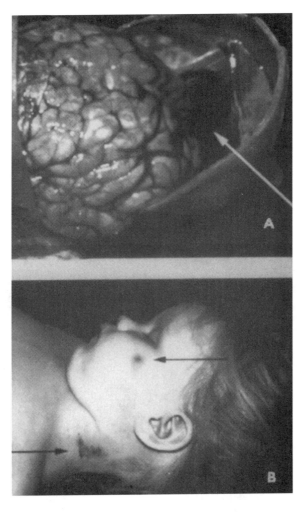

Pediatric Injuries. Abuse. Child reported to have fallen from a chair to the floor. A. Subdural and subarachnoid hemorrhages (white arrow). B. Abrasions and contusions (black arrows). Retinal hemorrhages were also present. The history did not fit this case of shaking injuries.

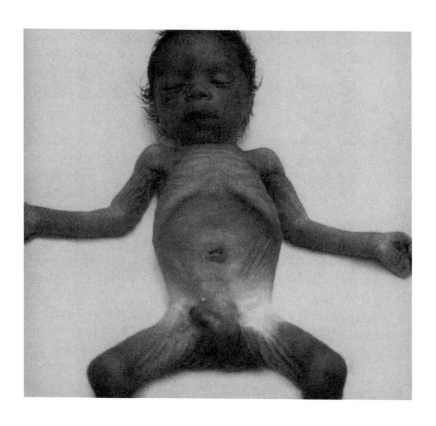

Pediatric Injuries. Neglect. This child died of malnutrition. Note powder remnants indicative of maternal care.

Appendix B: Medical Terminology

Adenoma - a benign tumor composed of glandular elements

Adhesion - fibrous tissue (scarring) which connects one structure to another as a response to disease or injury

ADP - adenosine diphosphate; an enzyme which forms, along with organic phosphate, as a result of hydrolysis of adenosine triphosphate, and is produced During muscle contraction

AIDS - Acronym for "acquired immune deficiency syndrome"; a disease caused by a retrovirus and characterized by severe immunosuppression associated with unusual infections, tumors and neurologic changes

Allele - one of several alternate forms of a gene occupying a s p e c i f i c locus on a chromosome

Alveoli - air sacs in the lungs

Ambulatory - able to walk

Anastomosis - a joining together

Aneurysm - an outpouching of a blood vessel or structure

Angina pectoris - chest pain without death of heart muscle

Angiography - an x-ray study of blood vessels by dye

Anoxia - no oxygen

Antecubital fossa - the space on the arm in front of the elbow

Antemortem - before death

Anterior - in front of

Anthracosis - black pigment from coal or cigarette smoke

Anthropophagia - insect and animal eating of the body after   death

Apnea - a suspension of breathing. A specific form occurs only during sleep and is referred to as sleep apnea.

Arachnoid - a delicate web-like covering of the brain and spinal   cord

Arrhythmia - abnormal heart beat

Arteriolonephrosclerosis - small blood vessel disease of the   kidneys

Arteriovenous malformation - a vascular malformation consisting of a tangle of many, abnormally tortuous, misshapen vessels

Artery - a blood vessel which takes blood away from the heart

Arteriosclerosis - thickening of arterial walls, "hardening of the arteries"

Ascites - accumulation of fluid in the abdomen

Asphyxia - lack of oxygen in the blood

Atelectasis - collapse of a lung

Atherosclerosis - thickening of arterial walls by fatty deposits

ATP - adenosine triphosphate; a nucleotide compound occurring in all cells where it represents energy storage

Atrium - one of two chambers in the heart which accepts blood from either the lungs or the rest of the body

Atrophy - wasting away

Autolysis - degeneration of cells and tissues after death

Avulsed - torn away from

Barbiturate - a group or organic compounds, derived from barbituric acid, which act as depressants of the central nervous system (ex: amytal, pentothal, phenobarbital, seconal)

Benzoylecgonine - a metabolite of cocaine

Bifurcation - a division into two branches

Bilirubin - a breakdown product of red blood cells

Bradycardia - slow heart beat; pulse rate less than 60 beats per minute

Bronchi - the breathing tubes between the trachea and the lungs

Bronchioles - smaller divisions of the bronchi

Bronchopneumonia - infection of the lung beginning in the bronchiole

Bulbar conjuctiva - coats anterior portion of eyeball

Calcification - turning hard by the development of calcium salts

Cancer - malignant growth

Cannabis - marijuana

Capillary - the smallest blood vessel connecting arteries and veins

Carbohydrates - starches and sugars

Cardiac - pertaining to the heart

Cardiac tamponade - blood filling the pericardial sac and compressing the heart

Cardiomegaly - increased size of the heart

Cardiomyopathy - a general term designating primary myocardial disease

Cardiopulmonary resuscitation (CPR) - literally heart-lung resuscitation; a sequence of methods and procedures that one learns to attempt to bring back unconscious individuals to full consciousness

Cardiorespiratory - heart and lungs

Cardiovascular - heart and blood vessels

Cecum - the first part of the large bowel (colon) where the small bowel attaches and the appendix is located

Cerebral - brain

Cholecystectomy - surgical removal of the gallbladder

Cholelithiasis - gallstones

Chordae tendineae - strings of tissue connecting heart valves to papillary muscles in the heart wall

Circle of Willis - union of anterior and posterior cerebral arteries which form a connection at the base of the brain

Cirrhosis - scarring of the liver complicating alcoholism

Coagulation - the process of clotting

Cocaine - hydrochloride of an alkaloid obtained from erythroxyin coca. A habit forming drug. Also used as a local and topical anesthetic on mucous membranes

Codeine - an alkaloid obtained from opium or synthetically from morphine. Used commonly for cough suppression; also used as an analgesic or sedative resembling morphine

Colon - the large bowel, between the small bowel and the anus

Coma - unresponsive condition

Congenital - born with

Congestion - accumulation of blood

Conjunctiva - the thin membrane lining the eyelid and eyeball

Connective tissue - the supporting tissue between structures

Consolidation - becoming firm

Contrecoup - opposite the point of impact

Coronal - the plane across the body from side to side

Coup - at the point of impact

Cribriform plate - the thin, perforated medial portion of the horizontal plate of the ethmoid bone

Cutaneous - skin

Cyanosis - the dusky discoloration of the skin due to a lack of oxygen

Cyst - a hollow structure with a lining filled with a liquid or a semiliquid substance

DNA (deoxyribonucleic acid) - a nucleic acid; genetic material for most organisms, including humans

Decubitus ulcer - an ulcer formed on the skin from pressure

Dementia - loss of intellectual function

Dermatome - the distribution of a nerve on the exterior of the body

232

Diabetes mellitus - a disease in which the body cannot use sugar because insulin is not being adequately produced by the pancreas

Diastolic - the lower of the two values in a blood pressure

Dilantin - trademark for preparation of diphenylhydantoin sodium used as an anticonvulsant especially in treatment of epilepsy

Dilaudid - trademark for preparations of hydromorphine hydrochloride used to relieve pain

Distal - away from the point of insertion

Duodenum - the first part of the small bowel

Dura mater - the tough, thick membrane located between the brain and the skull

-ectomy - excision of

Ecchymoses - hemorrhages beneath the skin (larger than petechiae)

Edema - the accumulation of fluid in cells and tissues

Electrocardioversion - an attempt at cardiopulmonary resuscitation by electrical shook

Emaciation - generalized wasting away

Emphysema - lung disease where there is retention of air because of alveoli damage

Endometrium - the inner lining of the uterus

Epidural - over the dura

Esophagus - the structure connecting the mouth to the stomach

Ethmoid bone - small, sieve-like spongy bone located in the nasal fossa

Etiology - the cause of a disease

Exsanguination - marked internal or external loss of blood

Fibrillation - very rapid irregular heart beat

Fibrosis - formation of fibrous or scar-like tissue

Flexion - the act of bending a structure

Forensic pathology - the legal applications to the field of pathology

Foramen magnum - the hole at the base of the skull through which the spinal cord passes

Fossa - a furrow or shallow depression

Fracture - a broken bone. Can have several varieties such as:

  simple - bone is broken with no external wound

  compound - bone is broken with an external wound leading down to the fracture site or having fragments of bone protrude through the skin

  comminuted - bone is broken or splintered into pieces

  depressed - when a piece of skull is broken and driven inwards

Gastrocnemius - the calf muscle

Gastrointestinal - pertaining to stomach and intestine

Genome - complete genetic information within a cell or carried by an organism

Gland - a structure made up of cells which secrete a substance

Glucose - sugar

Granular - a "lumpy bumpy" surface

Granuloma - a tumor-like growth caused by an infection

Halothane - a fluorinated hydrocarbon used during induction of anesthesia

Hematoma - a mass (collection) of blood

-hemo - blood

Hemorrhage - abnormal external or internal discharge of blood

Hemosiderin - an iron containing pigment derived from hemoglobin from disintegration of red blood cells

Hepatomegaly - increased size of the liver

Hepatic - pertaining to the liver

Herniation - the protrusion of a structure into another space

Heroin - a narcotic derived from morphine

Hybridization - complementary pairing of nucleic acid strands

Hyperglycemia - increased sugar in the blood

Hyperplastic - increased number

Hypertension - high blood pressure; as in hypertensive heart disease

Hyperthermia - increased body temperature

Hypertrophy - enlargement

Hypothermia - decreased body temperature

Hypoglycemia - decreased sugar in the blood

Hypovolemia - diminished blood volume

Hysterectomy - surgical removal of the uterus

Ileum - the third and most distal part of the small bowel

Infarction - death of tissue from a lack of blood

Inferior - below

Inflammation - a local response to cellular injury

Infraorbital - below the eye

Intercostal - between the ribs

Interstitial tissue - the supporting tissue within an organ - not the
     functioning cell

Intestines - the bowels

Intima - the innermost structure

Ischemia - decreased blood flow

-itis - inflammation

Jaundice - yellow discoloration of the skin from a buildup of bilirubin in
     the body

Jejunum - the second part of the small bowel

Korsakoff's Syndrome - named after a Russian neurologist, it describes a personality characterized by psychosis with polyneuritis (inflammation of 2 or more nerves), delirium, insomnia, illusions, and hallucinations. Frequently occurs as a sequel to chronic alcoholism.

Langer's Lines - structural orientation of the fibrous tissue of the skin which forms natural cleavage lines present in all body areas but visible only in certain areas such as the creases of   thepalm

Laparotomy - surgical incision into the abdomen

Larynx - the upper part of trachea containing the vocal cords

Leukemia - cancer of the blood forming organs and cells

Ligament - thick tissue joining bones and cartilage

Ligature - a thread or wire for tying a blood vessel or other structure in order to constrict it

Livor mortis - settling of blood after death

Locus - location of a gene on a chromosome

Lumen - the inside of a hollow organ or blood vessel

Lymph - the clear fluid which drains from the body's tissues

Lymphocyte - a white blood cell that makes an immune response against a foreign molecule (antigen)

Lymphoma - cancer of the lymph system

Lymph node - nodules of tissue along the lymph drainage system

Marijuana - obtained from leaves and flowers of the indian hemp plant (Cannabis sativa), an intoxicating, excitant drug

Marfan's Syndrome - a congenital disorder of connective tissue characterized by abnormal length of extremities, especially of fingers and toes, subluxation of the lens, cardiovascular abnormalities (commonly dilatation of the ascending aorta), and other deformities

Mastectomy - surgical removal of the breast

Mastoid - the area of the skull behind the ear

Media - the middle layer of a blood vessel

Medial - the middle

Membrane - the lining tissue within a structure or between two structures

Meningitis - inflammation of the coverings of the brain

Mesentery - the structure which supports the intestines

Metabolite - a breakdown product of a drug or chemical

Methodone - a synthetic compound with pharmacologic action similar to morphine and heroin; used as a substitute narcotic in the treatment of heroin addiction

Mitral valve - the valve between the left atrium and ventricle in the heart

Molecular biology - a branch of biology that studies the simplest or elementary organization of living organism

Morphine - main alkaloid found in opium; widely used as an analgesic and sedative

Myocardium - heart muscle

Myocardial infarct - death of heart muscle from blockage of a coronary artery

Nanogram (ng) - one billionth of a gram (10^{-9} gram)

Necrosis - degeneration and death of cells and tissues during life

Neoplasia - tumor or growth

Occipital - concerning the back part of the head

Osmolarity - concentration of osmotically active particles in solution

Osteon - basic unit of structure of compact bone, with concentrically arranged lamellae around a haversian canal

-otomy - incision into

Palpebrae Conjuctiva - covers undersurface of lids

Pancreas - the organ behind the stomach which produces insulin

Papillary muscles - muscle bundles which control the heart valves

Parenchyma - the functional tissue of an organ

PCR - polymerase chain reaction; technique for amplifying specific DNA regions by repetitious cycles of separating DNA strands, binding of primers, and extension or polymerization of new DNA strands

Penetration - into a structure

Perforation - through a structure

Peri - prefix meaning around as in periumbilical (around the umbilicus or "belly-button")

Pericardial sac - the sac surrounding the heart

Perineum - the area of the body which includes the external genitalia and the anus

Peritoneal cavity - abdominal cavity

Peritoneum - the thick tissue lining the abdominal cavity

Perivascular - around blood vessels

Petechiae - pinpoint hemorrhages

Pharynx - the structure at the back of the nose and mouth before the esophagus and larynx

238

Phencyclidene - an anesthetic

Phenothiazines - used in treatment of psychological disorders

Pinna - the external ear

Pleura - lining the lung or inside the chest

Pleural space - space between the lung and the chest wall

Polymerase - a protein which catalyzes large molecule formation

Polymorphism - simultaneous occurrence in the genome of different forms of an allele

Posterior - behind or back

Postmortem - after death

Primer - small portion of double-stranded DNA used to initiate synthesis of new strands

Probe - a defined nucleic acid fragment, radioactively or c h e m i c a l l y labeled, used to locate a nucleic acid sequence by complementary based pairing (hybridization)

Prone - lying on the front

Protein C or S Deficiency - protein C and S are vitamin K dependent clotting factors. Activation of either protein C or S makes them potent anticoagulants. Hence, a deficiency of either one causes an individual to be prone to clot or thrombus formation

Proximal - towards the point of insertion or the main part of the body

Purging - the decomposed bodily fluids which come out the nose and mouth

Pyelonephritis - inflammation of kidney substance and pelvis

RNA (ribonucleic acid) - involved in protein synthesis and is the genetic material for some viruses

Renal - kidney

Rheumatic Disease - pertaining to rheumatism which is a general term for acute and chronic conditions characterized by soreness and stiffness of muscles, pain in joints and associated structures

Rigor mortis - stiffening of the muscles after death

Sagittal - a plane across the body from front to back

Salpingo-oopherectomy - surgical removal of the fallopian tubes and ovaries

Saponify - to convert into soap

Sarcoma - a malignant tumor of the soft tissue

Scapula - large, flat, triangular bone which forms posterior part of the shoulder

Seizure - sudden attack of pain, of a disease, or of certain symptoms

Septicemia - bacteria in the blood system with signs and symptoms of disease

Shock - inadequate circulating blood volume because of either a loss or redistribution of blood

Sinus - a cavity in a bone of the skull usually communicating with the nostrils and containing air

Skeletonization - removal of soft parts of the body leaving only the skeleton

Small bowel - the small intestine; extends from the stomach to the colon

Soft tissue - fat or supporting tissue

Splenectomy - surgical removal of the spleen

Stenosis - narrowing

Stillborn - dead at birth

Subarachnoid - beneath the arachnoid

Subcutaneous marbling - the external black discoloration of blood
vessels which appears during decomposition

Subclavian/Subclavicular - under the clavicle or collarbone

Subdural - beneath the dura

Subluxation - bones which partially slip out of joint

Superior - above

Supine - lying on the back with face upward

Supraorbital - above the eye

Suture - joints in the skull where the bones come together

Syncope - fainting

Systolic - the higher of the two values in a blood pressure

Tachycardia - fast heart beat

Talwin - trademark for pentazocine lactate used as an analgesic

Tardieu spots - small hemorrhages from ruptured blood vessels on the
extremities occurring after a body has been in a dependent position

Temporal Bone - a bone on both sides of the skull at its base

Thoracic cavity - chest cavity

Thoracotomy - surgical incision into chest cavity

Thorax - chest

Thorazine™ - a central nervous system depressant; also employed as a
sedative and an antiemetic

Thymus - single organ located in mediastinal cavity anterior to and
above the heart. Important in development of immune response in
newborns

Trachea - tubal structure between larynx and bronchi; "wind pipe"

Tricuspid valve - valve between right atrium and right ventricle in the
heart

Tricyclic antidepressants - a group of compounds used to treat depression by causing elevation in mood, increased physical activity and mental alertness. Some common ones are amitriptyline, desipramine, and trazodone

Tuberculosis - an infectious disease caused by the tubercle bacillus, Mycobacterium tuberculosis, and characterized pathologically by inflammatory infiltrations, formation of tubercles, caseating granulomas, necrosis, abscesses, fibrosis, and calcification. Most commonly affects respiratory system but can affect other parts of the body

Umbilicus - technical term for "belly-button"

Ureter - the structure which takes urine from the kidney to the urinary bladder

Varix (Varices) - enlarged dilated vein(s) from a backup of blood - seen in alcoholics who have cirrhosis

Vasculature - the arrangement of veins in the body or any part of it, including their relationship and function

Vein - a blood vessel which returns blood to the heart

Ventricle - a chamber containing either blood or fluid (e.g., the heart has two ventricular chambers)

Vitreous humor - the fluid in the eye which gives the eye its shape

Wernicke's Syndrome - consists of defective memory, loss of sense of location, and confabulation. Seen in chronic alcoholics

INDEX

Jacket (bullet), 57

Lacerations, 87
Langer's lines (skin), 63
Lands-and-grooves, 6, 57
Ligature marks, 75
Livor mortis, 34
Loose contact gunshot wound, 58
LSD (lysergic acid diethylamide), 73

Malignant hyperthermia, 84
Malnutrition (children), 101
Manner of death, 31
Maryland, 2
Mechanism of death, 30
Medical examiner, 5
Microscopic examinations, 17
Missouri, 2
Missouri vs. Davis (DNA case), 123
Motor vehicle injuries, 88
    driver vs. passenger, 141
    occupants, 88
    pedestrians, 89-90
Mummification, 41
Myocarditis, 50

Natural death, 48-55
Negative autopsy, 55
Neglect (children), 101

Viral infestions,
    heart, 50
    lungs, 54
Vitreous humor, 16, 36, 101

Water in the lungs (drowning), 79-80, 145
Weapon type,
    general, 137
    knife, 139-141
Witness (scene), 26

X-rays,
    child abuse, 99
    fire deaths, 82
    identification, 44, 46
    live birth determination (case), 183

Zero-order kinetics (in ethyl alcohol metabolism), 67